To Johnnie &
Debra —
We are rooting for you!
Congrats on a healthy,
permanent relationship!
Blessings,

HIGH FIVE
Love Never Fails

5 Key Principles For The Forever Family

Ron, Catherine, and Brandon Tijerina

ISBN-13: 978-0-9889382-1-2

Printed in the
United States of America

Cover Design: Dream Pump
Interior Design: Dream Pump

Dedication

To our family.

Acknowledgements

Love Never Fails. 1 Corinthians 13:8

We give all glory and honor to our Savior Jesus Christ for carrying us through our darkest hours and setting us on solid ground. He is the true author of our story and these principles.

Writing this book was an adventure for our family; then again, the past 27 years have been an adventure! Our children Blake, Brandon and Bria, our daughters-in-law Jaclyn and Andrea, and our grandchildren Mya and Dawson all joined us on this trek. Each of them contributed to this book in different ways. You will see their fingerprints on every page. Their perseverance, patience, and encouragement made this book a reality.

Nobody becomes successful alone. The team who organized, edited, designed and built a process for this project is amazing – THANK YOU! We could not have done it without your help. Finally, on behalf of the Tijerina family, we want to convey our deepest gratitude to the hundreds of people who have poured their time, love and prayers into helping our family succeed.

We are rooting for you!

The Tijerina Family

If you do not have the privilege of knowing these precious people and having heard this amazing family share their struggle and determination to keep their marriage and their family strong, do yourself a favor and read this book! Learn their heart and their journey from imprisonment to freedom. If you are struggling to find ways to keep your own precious family strong, read this book. You will find your own heart stirred with conviction and determination.

- Cosette Bowles
(*Executive Director, ANTHEM Strong Families*)

In love and life Ron and Catherine Tijerina are truly the salt and light that this world so desperately needs. HIGH FIVE, Love Never Fails is a must read for any couple, man or woman who wants to strengthen their relationships, nurture their marriage and transform their lives together!

- Dr. Randell Turner
(*Author of Rescuing the Rogue: Restoring True Relational Intimacy for Men & The Rogue Intimacy Curriculum*)

Ron and Cathy's gripping story of relational tenacity and grace, against all odds, inspires and teaches. **Caution** — their profound lessons have the power to impact you deeply, as they have us.

- Sherod Miller, PhD and Phyllis A. Miller, PhD
(*Co-Developers of the Couple Communication Program and CEO, Interpersonal Communication Programs, Inc.*)

One of the deepest needs of humans is to be connected to the ones we love. Ron and Cathy's book, "High Five, Love Never Fails" shares really personal stories and professional insight into how to connect and be fulfilled in your relationships. This book is a MUST read book for all couples and families. I couldn't put it down!

- Maggie Russell
(Executive Director Nat'l Assoc. for Relationship & Marriage Education)

Table of Contents

Prison Saved Our Family

Ron Tijerina

If friendship was a cardinal virtue, then I was about to receive sainthood in the lobby outside of the ladies' dressing room.

I love my wife and my three children, and for more than 20 years I have been committed to helping our family grow and be healthy and success-ful, even from behind bars. I have been sent to prison twice for a crime I did not commit and have served 15 years in Ohio's prison system. I have been attacked, accused, rejected, and broken.

I am currently in a department store, waiting for my wife outside of the ladies' dressing room, and I am happy I am able to be here. She is my best friend.

Families are built with friendship. The fullest expression of true love is really true friendship. It is the ability to share the secret, vulnerable things in our hearts with another person and know that we can trust them to accept us. When we are faithful to others and demonstrate loyalty to them, we build the trust that helps the friendship to grow. When we do things together, we demonstrate the fact that the "us" in the relationship means more than "me" or "you."

When offenses come, as they inevitably do, we can learn to look past the hurt in our heart that seems so large and show love to the other people in our family who are hurting as well, and probably more than we are. And when someone or something comes to strike a mighty blow to our family, the strength that comes from learning to love each other every day and making those little choices that matter will carry us through the big trials of life.

I am currently choosing to build my relationship with my wife by doing something that matters to her. I am also trying to look as cool as a 40 something year old man can look while standing outside of the ladies' dressing room.

Practicing this way of life will make the bonds of your family permanent. Learning how to love your family and help them to grow strengthens the whole family so that they will be there when you desperately need their support as well. This is what it is to practice the High Fives – the principles that we discovered in the midst of incarceration, separation and despair. These principles helped us to rise from our circumstances, become strong, and help thousands of other families to do the same.

I learned to be there for my wife and children, even from behind bars, for 15 years. I am here for my wife right now, just outside the ladies' dressing room, while she tries on 4 more outfits.

Success is something everyone wants, but very few people understand how to achieve. Personal happiness, productivity, healthy bodies, healthy relationships, creating a legacy – all these things come from one source: a healthy family. A healthy family is proven to benefit every individual in it and to give them success, joy and peace in their lives. A family with a mother and father who love each other and work to make the family successful is the atmosphere that allows children to grow to their full potential. It is the foundation for achievement and happiness. Success in life comes from success in your family. The problem is that most marriages and families are not successful, and many of them fail.

My marriage became an example to the other men in prison, and they asked my wife to start visiting their families to encourage them. This was even before I enjoyed shopping with my wife.

There is a great myth that is widely accepted as a truth - the myth that perfect relationships exist. Men and women chase after this illusion as if it is their promised inheritance. What is the result?
The quest for a perfect relationship is a constant source of dissatisfaction; no person, no relationship is perfect. In the 1950s, the perfect family myth was born. It has been such a powerful idea that people have

chased after it for generations. But many of today's young people have become so disillusioned that when the fairy tale of a perfect family burst like a soap bubble, they give up on marriage and family altogether.

At this point, I think the perfect shopping trip might be a myth too. Two more outfits to go, outside the ladies' dressing room.

The truth is that healthy families are possible. They are not perfect, but they are real, and they can be built. A broken and dysfunctional family can change and grow into a strong, healthy, vibrant family. Our family made the journey from suffering and shattered to strong and healthy. Our family is not perfect, but we learned and practiced the skills to make it permanent.

I have committed to achieving the greater good for my family and my marriage - even if I am the only husband standing outside the dressing room.

When we started on our journey together more than 26 years ago, we did not have the skills to build a healthy, successful marriage and family, and we suffered. While I was in prison, we learned the High Five principles, which made it possible for us to actually grow closer and stronger through the difficulties that could have consumed us.

I really hope the dressing room has not consumed Cathy…

Cathy and I now work with our adult sons full-time to strengthen families in our home state of Ohio and around the world. Over the last year alone, we have reached into the lives of more than one hundred thousand families. We know what it has taken to bring health and wholeness into our own family, and we've seen these same principles work in the lives of countless others.

Finally, I am done standing outside the ladies' dressing room! "Looks great, Cathy! You are beautiful. They will love that dress at the White House!"

We have come so far. From a suffering young family with a prison sentence, poverty and welfare to helping so many others to have success in their families, and receiving recognition by the White House. If your family is hurting too, please let us help you. Practicing the High Five principles teaches you how to strengthen your family in the midst of suffering, improving your family's health so that no matter what you face, you can face it together and be successful.

The High Five principles can transform your family just like it transformed ours.

You may even find yourself happy to be standing outside of a dressing room, too, someday!

Chapter 1

Ron – Your House, Your Home

Bright white lights illuminated a quaint-looking, older farmhouse. "We're here!" I announced as I pulled up the grassy drive. The grand, front porch had an oversized swing on one end and four hanging baskets overflowing with sweet-smelling pastel flowers on the other. It was such a welcomed sight.

I opened the side door of the van and looked into three pairs of sleepy, squinting eyes. Bria, my eight-year old daughter, along with Mya, my four year-old granddaughter, and Dawson, my two year-old grandson were all barely awake after our long journey. My wife, Cathy, got out of the front seat and paused to smile at me. I wondered if she knew how her smile filled my world with warmth. We began unloading the children and some of our vacation supplies. As we entered the house we were greeted by a shiny, cheerful kitchen with a large white table in the center. It was exactly what we had hoped for!

Cathy ushered the three children, who had suddenly become wide awake, into their bedrooms. As she moved up the stairs, ignoring the three part harmony of "but I'm not tired," I began my return to the car to get the rest of the supplies. As I did, I suddenly noticed a mouse on one of the kitchen chairs. I quickly looked back to make sure Cathy had not seen it. "Whew! All clear." I took the broom and swatted it outside.

Almost nothing evokes panic in Cathy, except the appearance of a mouse. I was determined that our family vacation would be fun and relaxing; unfortunately, my determination was not enough. As she walked back into the kitchen to help me, a second mouse ran across her path. She catapulted onto the dining room table with a bloodcurdling shriek. That was the war cry that set the stage for our vacation.

As it turns out, the first mouse I had ushered from the house didn't even dent the rodent population we were dealing with! My first thought was to flee, but we were in the midst of a sold out resort community and had

FRIENDSHIP

FAITHFULNESS

FORGIVENESS

FAIRNESS

FORTITUDE

no other lodging options for the week. Our choice was to stay or go home. Since our son and daughter-in-law were meeting us in a few days, we decided to stay.

We all armed ourselves with brooms and fly swatters so we could shoo the mice out of the rooms. Even Dawson had a fly swatter and was prepared to defend himself if necessary. Cathy insisted that we all sleep together in the one queen bed, so the mice would not attack the children in their sleep. Yes, all five of us! Throughout each night, Cathy and I took turns waiting for the dreaded attack of the mice. I caught more mice that week than I have ever caught in my life, and still they kept coming and coming! Nothing is more frustrating than focusing all of your energy on a goal that seems unattainable.

As a guest in that house, I was unable to do the things I knew could eradicate the problem. So, that week, I was a very frustrated warrior. The mice had become so accustomed to living there that they would just scurry right out in front of us. I was constantly on my guard, ready to swing at the next rodent that would appear on the counter, the couch or the chair. As the mice kept coming, Cathy walked around banging lids, carrying a broom, and looking for safe places to leap onto. It was an absolutely miserable time.

We were on high alert – code red. I chanted, "Danger, Will Robinson! Danger!" as a warning to others that a mouse had been seen. A stressful week of vigilance for combat, while my wife was constantly prepared for retreat, left us completely exhausted. "How did they let this get so bad?" we kept asking each other. For our inconvenience, the owners offered us an extra week free of charge. Living in defense mode for one week was more than enough for us! We declined their offer, and they refunded our money.

We all recognize the danger of allowing rodents to overtake our homes. It is not only undesirable, but also unhealthy. Most of us would never allow such an infestation. At the first sign of rodents, we would do everything humanly possible to get rid of them. We would go to the local, big box store and spend hundreds of dollars on traps, baits and devices to catch the mice. If that failed we would call for a professional extermi- nator. None of us would choose to live in this situation.

Sadly, the same is not true for the other types of infestations that are destroying the health of millions of families worldwide. Selfishness, dishonor, disrespect, lust, cheating, lying and other nuisances attack our marriages and families. Infestations, like these, are often ignored right up to the time when everyone finally recognizes them as unac- ceptable and someone decides to flee. As these things creep in and find little or no resistance, they grow and multiply. When everyone must be constantly prepared for combat, it doesn't take long for exhaustion and apathy to enter into your relationships.

The vacation home looked amazing on the internet and wonderful in person. It could have been a great vacation spot without the pests. It wasn't the location, the attractions or our time together that defined that vacation. The stress of living in constant anticipation of combat is what we remember.

Think about your home. Not the structure where you live, but really think about your home. The condition of your home is defined by the culture created by your relationships. Is it a peaceful place to be? Is it a place that fosters emotional, mental, spiritual and physical health? Or is it a type of battleground? Do you find yourself preparing for conflict ev- ery day or walking on eggshells to avoid confrontation? If you find that your home has become infested with things that are robbing you of your relational health, your joy, and your energy, then it is time for a culture change in your home.

If that had been our home, we would have pulled out all the stops to regain control of it. We would have called in the experts, bought every rodent control product available, and we would have cleaned out that house. But, since it wasn't our home, we just walked away from the house and decided never, ever to go there again. We were so happy to arrive back at our home after that trip. Home was even sweeter than we remembered it. As you change your plan from ignoring the problems, to controlling the problems, and finally to eliminating the problems, the High Five will give you the tools and skill sets you need to become successful at the MOST IMPORTANT assignment of your life - restoring your marriage and family. No matter what you are going through, or have been through, you can create the experience of "home sweet home" in your life. We can show you how.

FRIENDSHIP

FAITHFULNESS

FORGIVENESS

FAIRNESS

FORTITUDE

Cathy - At the White House

It was May 13, 2012. We were about to get a phone call.

Ron and I are co-founders of The RIDGE Project, a non-profit organization that is devoted to building a legacy of strong marriages and families. In 2010, we received the Impact Award from Smart Marriages® for our work with incarcerated fathers and their families. In 2011, The RIDGE Project was identified as a "Best Practice" from the National Fatherhood Initiative, the Department of Justice and the Department of Health and Human Services.

The phone rang. We were asked to come to Washington, D.C. to be recognized by the White House as a "Champion of Change" in the field of fatherhood. We were overjoyed! We founded The RIDGE Project in 2000 with our dedication to serve families and our desire to reach people and train them to address the everyday challenges they face with honor, discipline and integrity. We work with all kinds of families, from the affluent to the impoverished. We teach them what we have learned in our own lives, and share the lessons we learned from the hardships we suffered. Our family grew strong in spite of the devastation which could have ripped it apart.

There and Back Again - TWICE!

We got an unexpected call once before, with even bigger news than the call from the White House.

4

Ron picked up the phone after I dropped it and it crashed to the floor. It was our attorney. He said that Ron's release from prison had been overturned, and that Ron would have to go back and serve out his original sentence of 14-25 years. There had been no proof of Ron's guilt, and the judge expressed doubt concerning the verdict, but through an unusual series of circumstances, Ron was convicted anyway.

When we were first married, our family was the poster child for failure. When our sons were very little and our marriage was rocky, Ron was sent to prison for 14-25 years. Socially, I raised the boys by myself, living on public assistance for 8 years, visiting Ron as often as I could, and dealing with a mountain of emotional turmoil. We lived in an older trailer with tires holding the roof down. A relative, "Aaron," had made the accusation which sent my husband to prison. When Ron was finally released after ten years, he was home for only six months before we got the devastating news that he would have to return to prison and serve out the remainder of his sentence. Our daughter, Bria, would be born while her Daddy was in prison and would not even live with him until she was nearly four years old.

> The precious gold that became our marriage was forged in the fiery furnace of hardship, injustice, separation and suffering.

We were not exactly White House material when we started out.

The precious gold that became our marriage was forged in the fiery furnace of hardship, injustice, separation and suffering. We learned how to build a solid foundation for our family, a place of safety for our children, and a marriage that, even while separated by bars, was an example to those around us. We started out as low as you can get, but God raised us up high. We learned the High Five principles that changed our marriage and saved our family.

We want to teach you these same principles, so that your family can rise above whatever obstacles you are facing, too.

The High Five -
Friendship, Faithfulness, Forgiveness, Fairness, and Fortitude

We have been helping families heal and become whole for more than twenty years. We have seen families that were extremely dysfunctional and broken almost beyond repair overcome their challenges to live in peace, harmony and friendship with each other. So over the next few pages, we're going to share with you what we have learned. Some of this may sound familiar, but some of it is going to surprise you and challenge your core beliefs. That's okay. But we do promise that what we have learned and put into this book will show you a new way of living and will create the possibility for the kind of wholeness, joy, and success that you, like most people, may not even believe is possible. You may be thinking it is ridiculous to imagine that even the most fragmented family could achieve genuine wholeness. We are going to challenge you to believe in the ridiculous, because with God, all things are possible!

How Happy is Your Marriage?

Is your marriage vibrant? Is it strong, permanent, and able to withstand the test of time, the terrible twos, and the challenge of raising teens? That is what we all want and hope for when we get married, but for most people, marriage ends up becoming something far less than what we envisioned. Through our work, we regularly meet with people whose families and marriages have suffered neglect and gone stale. Is that your family and marriage – looking full and put together on the outside, but stale, neglected, and empty on the inside? Perhaps your marriage has been weakened by poverty, bitterness, or anger. Or has it been devastated by an affair, addiction, or abuse? Do you feel that divorce is inevitable? Do you feel that ending the marriage is the only road to happiness? Have you been down that road before, and don't want to go down it again?

If you find yourself pondering these questions, you are not alone. We hear every day from people just like you, people who want their marriage and their family to be more, to be better, to be happy and fun again – or maybe for the first time. Most are asking themselves this question, "Is marriage worth it?"

Is Marriage Outdated?

Most of us are familiar with the children's story "The Emperor's New Clothes." In this story, a deceitful tailor made imaginary clothes for a foolish king and told him that everyone else could see the clothes. The king pretends to see them too, until a little boy told him that he was really naked.

Many young people today feel that marriage is like the pretend clothes of the emperor. These young people are telling us something profound. They are saying, "You can pretend family is some great thing, but look around." According to the US Center for Disease Control and Prevention (CDC), more than half of today's marriages fail.

The common perception is that married couples fall into two groups (both of which include people wishing they weren't married at all): those who will choose to get out of one marriage and then into another, or those who will suffer most of their life in a marriage they don't know how to escape. All too often, this perception is reality, and the children caught in these relationships end up resenting their parents while the parents see their children as a burden. Young people today are telling us the emperor has no clothes – happy marriage is an oxymoron and a cruel joke. We can't not listen.

But that doesn't mean that everyone should just divorce, or put their children up for adoption. It doesn't mean that we should take a vow to never marry. It especially doesn't mean that we should give up on the relationships we are already in. It does mean we should embrace the power to change it.

What is a Healthy Family . . . Exactly?

FRIENDSHIP

FAITHFULNESS

FORGIVENESS

FAIRNESS

FORTITUDE

Whether we know it or not, healthy family is the thing we all want and hope for. No one gets into a relationship thinking, "I really hope this will fail." So what does it mean to be a healthy family? Does it mean having both parents married and living together in the same house? Does it mean spending time together on the weekends? Does it mean having a game night when everyone stops their lives and laughs together? The problem is that a lot of families don't know the answer. There are reality TV shows on how families interact and magazines about celebrity family drama, but when it comes to helping our own families, most people have no idea how to communicate or even maintain relationships with each other.

So many families appear to have it all together, but behind closed doors no one talks or everybody yells; husband and wife don't sleep in the same room, and parents have no idea what is going on in the lives of their children. If this sounds like you or someone you know, please don't give up. Marriage really can be your greatest source of happiness, peace, and fulfillment. Statistically speaking, because of both the life circumstances we were thrust into and the ones we unwisely created, we ourselves should not still be married, and our children should be addicts, abusers, and inmates. We defied the odds.

Over the years, we have worked with thousands of folks with seemingly impossible barriers to having a happy family – incarceration, abuse, infidelity, addiction, and selfishness. They have overcome their obstacles and made it. Countless couples now enjoy beautiful, healthy, and thriving relationships – and you can too!

Marriage and Family

So here's where we start. We have to recognize that to be married and have a family is normal, healthy, and good. People in successful marriages and well-functioning families can achieve high levels of personal energy, great health, financial well-being, deeply satisfying relationships, work that is fulfilling, and just about every other good thing that life can bring.

How Do You Become a Healthy Family?

A healthy family doesn't just happen by accident. It isn't magic. It doesn't just happen to lucky people. Creating a committed, responsible relationship takes effort. It is a way of living and relating to others.

Is This a Self-help Technique?

Using individual self-help techniques to heal a family does not work because the root of family problems is selfishness. Focusing your energy to get "what I need and what I want" does not translate into building a strong family. Instead, it often builds more discontentment and more expectations based on fantasy about how others should meet our needs.

Our Model is Different... and It Works!

What if each member of a family would think more about what the others' needs and wants are? How different would the family dynamic be if no one was selfish (taking the easy path), but were all working together to help each other become more successful as individuals and as a vital part of the family unit? The dream of a strong, healthy family can be realized even in the most difficult circumstances.

Is Having a Happy Marriage Just a Fairy Tale?

So let's face this "emperor with no clothes." We agree with young adults who tell us that an unhealthy family experience cannot bring the good that we are talking about. In fact, if you had to choose between a hopelessly unhealthy family relationship and being single, we believe a single life would indeed be better than a marriage doomed to failure. Being married and having children when the whole thing is a miserable drudge that prevents you from being successful is not worth it. There is nothing about you that should make you feel compelled to be in a life that could not possibly bring you happiness.

But this is not the choice you face. The truth is that healthy marriages and families are possible for almost everyone. Not only are they possible, they are real. We have one, even though at one point in our lives everyone was telling us that we could not possibly be happy together. Great marriages and families are not only reserved for fairy tales or people who kiss frogs, counting on the miracle of a prince. Thriving marriages and families can be achieved, and more importantly, relationships that seem wrecked can be healed, made whole and full of joy!

Our Family Was Made Whole and Yours Can Be Too

As our family overcame 15 years of incarceration, we discovered some basic principles to having a healthy, strong marriage and family. These principles have helped thousands of families. They can help your family too. The investment in your family is the best investment you can make, and the return on this investment is measureless. Your family can experience the peace and stability and joy that you want, but are not sure how to find.

Our family suffered so much, yet from that suffering, we grew strong and whole. We are sharing our story with you in hopes that what we learned and what drew us together will help you as well.

Our Family's Story

As we began our journey as a new family in 1986, we had no idea how hard we were about to fight to keep our family together. When our sons were two and four years old, Ron was sent to prison for a crime he did not commit. For the next fifteen years, the battles that raged threatened to tear our family apart. We realized that if we wanted to survive, we would have to purposefully invest in what mattered most to us. As we began to focus our energy towards our family, something amazing began to happen. In spite of the hardships, together we began to thrive. We discovered principles that can strengthen families to withstand suffering and heal damaged and broken relationships.

Over the past 20 years we have been applying these principles in our daily lives. They worked for us and have become the foundation for an award-winning, nationally recognized program, (offered through the RIDGE Project), that has helped tens of thousands of families.

You Can Succeed Too!

We all want to be successful. We want to be healthy. We want financial well-being. We want to be really effective in our chosen work. We want to enjoy the good things in life. We want these things, and we work hard to achieve them. However, our success shouldn't come at the expense of other people's success. In fact, the more we invest in other people, the more successful we become. We will show you how to invest in your family and enjoy extraordinary success as you do so. We are proposing a win-win!

Our own family has suffered through trials and tribulations. We have gone through hardships that are beyond what most people can imagine. The suffering we have gone through has not torn us apart; we have been changed into something strong and permanent, a healthy family. We are pieces of a broken family that has been made whole. We have discovered the principles that have the power to transform and heal families. Your family can experience this healing too.

There is No Such Thing as Perfect!

We aren't perfect. We don't even imagine ourselves to be. One of Ron's favorite sayings is, "There is no such thing as perfect." We have, however, discovered the techniques necessary in order to have relationships that really work, and we apply them every day to keep those relationships healthy. These principles have transformed us and many others as we have applied them to real life challenges.
The new model of living as a truly successful family involves recognizing

FRIENDSHIP

FAITHFULNESS

FORGIVENESS

FAIRNESS

FORTITUDE

and developing skill in the five principles you will learn about in this book. We affectionately call them the High Five. The High Five will renew your family. These are the keys that we guarantee will transform your marriage and family. If you are ready to bring the dream of a happy, healthy family to life, this is exactly what you have been looking for. If you are ready to experience renewed life with your family in a whole new way, let the journey begin!

Chapter 2

Ron – Inspiration

"My brother is married." Just out of high school, I couldn't quite grasp the idea. My older brother, who had always seemed invincible, had fallen head over heels in love and was now married. I thought to myself, "Why would anyone want to settle down?" I watched him whirl his new bride across the dance floor while they laughed together. I took another bite of my cake and looked around the room to see who I would dance with next.

As I was scanning the room, my eyes caught a movement by the door. I turned, only slightly interested, to see who was coming into the room. Much to my surprise, the most beautiful woman I had ever seen walked into the reception hall. She was dressed in a white, belted suit with a skirt that hit just at her knees. Her long red hair was floating around her shoulders as she looked around the room for someone she knew. Her green eyes locked on mine and instantly, they flashed with recognition as her face broke into a warm smile. It was Cathy. My heart skipped a beat. I had known her for years, but this was the first time I had really seen her. How had I never realized how stunning she was? Every rational thought left my mind the moment she began to walk toward me. I said to myself, "WOW! I have got to make this girl mine!"

Why does a man take a wife? For the last 20 years, in seminars and in one-on-one trainings, we have been working with families to increase their functioning, joy and satisfaction. In that time, I have asked thousands of men this one simple question. The answers are almost always the same: "Friendship." "Helpmate." "Lover." "Desire for children." "To be made complete." All of these reasons are appropriate, but none of them is really true to this moment of your first encounter. From that first moment when I saw her differently, I did all I could to win Cathy over. I changed my routine and offered her the best I had. Now she is my wife of 27 years. Since then, I have won her over hundreds of times, and I still want to win her over today!

If you're a man, do you remember the very first moment you saw your lady? She was the woman of your dreams; you knew you had to do everything you could to get her attention. For some, this meant you went home and brushed your teeth in the middle of the day. For others, you pressed your favorite shirt, you brushed your hair, you dug out the cologne that you knew was irresistible - you did everything you could in order to put your best foot forward – to present yourself in the best possible light. You were focused and effective. You had one goal in mind: get that girl! And this made you want to be the best person you could possibly be.

What was it that she did that made you want to rise up and do things differently? Think carefully; it wasn't lust and it wasn't love. It was the possibility of being with her and sharing all the good things that are only possible with her. It was inspiration. She inspired you to go outside your normal routine, to be the best you could be; to become better than you were without her. The High Five points us to this level of inspiration. We all want the benefits of a good relationship and are inspired to become better by the challenge of getting them. This is why a man takes a wife; for inspiration.

Is this lacking in your relationship? Everyone wants to live an inspired life. But like most good things, it doesn't just happen because we say we want it. For most of us, we pursued and then attained. We "got the girl." It was a wonderful experience filled with happy memories. But then, somehow, it ended. The inspiration that drove us to do extraordinary things to win her heart, evaporated. We thought we had gotten all that was available and so the inspiration died. I want you to know that it doesn't have to be this way. If the inspiration in your life has gone out, the High Five principles can help.

Cathy - From Failure to Success

Inspired as we were in the earliest part of our relationship, we also managed to lose this passion. In fact, if someone wrote a book entitled, "How to Break Your Family and Make Your Marriage Fail," our early years would have been the case study. We didn't know how to communicate. We didn't know how to handle money. We didn't know how to be good parents or even what we wanted for our children. It was like we were living in a soap opera; things just happened and we had no idea what to do with them.

More than two decades after the shattering of our family by a wrongful conviction and fifteen years of incarceration, Ron and I serve as the Executive Directors of a multi-million dollar non-profit organization devoted to helping families become healthy. Our sons, Blake and Brandon have grown-up, and at present they work with us to reach out to families, teaching patterns of behavior that bring health and healing. Last year our organization reached over 100,000 people with a message of hope and a way to move forward in order to achieve what everyone wants - a healthy family.

It takes vision and hard work to run an organization. In the same way, it takes dedication and work to build a healthy family. Creating the vision for your family by knowing what it is that you want and knowing what you don't want is one of the critical first steps to beginning this process.

Miserably Ever After - Knowing What You Don't Want

A sweet looking older couple was making their way toward us in the grocery store. The husband was pushing the cart and shuffling along next to his wife. They had their heads bent toward each other as if they were sharing some secret just meant for the two of them. We smiled at each other and commented that we hoped that would be us in another 30 years.

Then they got close enough that we could hear what they were saying. "Woman!" he barked at her, "This is the third time you have me running down this aisle! With as much money as you spend in here, you ought to know where everything is without dragging me all over this store!" She just looked at the ground and kept walking. As they continued past us, we could hear him rant and rave at her for inconveniencing him. We

15

looked at each other and mutually agreed we would NOT be that couple in 30 years after all! Our hearts were heavy for the couple who appeared to have spent so many years of their lives together, but were actually so disconnected from each other. What had happened, we wondered, that had caused the distance to grow between them? Was it a single event they could not get past, or the buildup of years of grudges, disappointment, and anger? Whatever had happened, it was a sad commentary on their relationship. It was disheartening to see a married couple so at odds with each other that they didn't even notice all the onlookers as they made their way across a crowded grocery store, arguing and disrespecting each other.

What we just witnessed was, unfortunately, not unique. We were intrigued by this couple who we thought still liked each other, but then we realized we were mistaken and were saddened that they were just like so many other couples we had seen. Time after time we sit in a restaurant, airport, or mall and observe family members having heated conversations, or no conversation at all. It is not just couples who publicly show their discontentment and dysfunction; we see parents and children and whole families who are unhappy and fighting in public as well.

On a recent shopping trip, we witnessed a family quarrel. As a mother and her daughter, who appeared to be in her mid-twenties, entered a mobile phone store, their body language made it apparent they were arguing. The clerk greeted them and began looking something up on her computer for them. As she was checking the information on the computer, the mother and daughter began to raise their voices in a disagreement. It was not long before everyone in the store became spectators of the escalating dispute. We looked at the clerk who was serving us and asked if they had ever had to call the police. She assured us that each employee had call buttons at their stations to alert the police immediately if there was ever a problem. Less than two minutes later, the daughter reached across the other clerk and began hitting her mother! The clerk was doing her best to dodge the daughter's frantic swinging. She tried to get out of the middle of the altercation while the mother tried unsuccessfully to maintain some semblance of dignity and composure.

FRIENDSHIP

FAITHFULNESS

FORGIVENESS

FAIRNESS

FORTITUDE

The police arrived and the adult daughter was arrested and taken out in handcuffs. We could hardly believe we were watching this occur in a small rural town. This incident is just one example of the deteriorating health of more and more families. Who could have foreseen a time where we would need panic buttons in anticipation of family disputes over purchasing a cell phone? Surely there was a time in this family's history when they could not have imagined striking each other, especially at a public place in front of dozens of strangers. I will never forget the look of hurt and shame in the eyes of the mother as she walked out of that store alone. I knew that look well, because at one point in my life I was walking in shame, hurt and pain. But it wasn't always that way.

Cathy - The Story of our Struggle

When I was nineteen I was attending, on scholarships, a good college in central Ohio. I was studying with the hopes of one day becoming a lawyer. I was ambitious and I wanted to make a difference.

Along the way, I met Ron. We were both from the same small Midwestern town and actually knew each other as small children. His family had moved away after he was in first grade and then returned after we were both in high school. Ron and I didn't have the same social circles in high school. Ron mostly associated with people from the high school band and those who pursued fun. I was more involved in college prep activities.

Ron was a musician from a family of musicians, and was the drummer in a band. He was handsome and confident with a promising career in rock music. After my high school graduation, I saw Ron at his brother's wedding. In his white tuxedo, he was even more handsome! He was carefree and adventurous, and I guess I was looking for an adventure because we began dating. We both had our own goals and ambitions, but when we were together it was fun and exciting. We fell in love, as much as two nineteen year old people bent on fun and excitement are actually capable of love. We went to clubs, listened to Ron's band play, and everything else that goes with that lifestyle - sex, drugs, and alcohol.

FRIENDSHIP

FAITHFULNESS

FORGIVENESS

FAIRNESS

FORTITUDE

My parents disapproved of Ron and our relationship. My siblings were more or less indifferent toward Ron. Later in life, I realized that my family had many legitimate concerns. Even so, at the time, their disapproval was a source of frustration and ongoing irritation for me. I was set on proving I was not a child any longer, but an adult capable of making my own decisions about my relationships.

Before long, Ron and I were married and expecting our first child. At first, nothing very much changed. House parties pretty much replaced clubbing, but most everything else seemed to stay the same. We didn't realize at that moment that we had almost systematically set ourselves up for failure.

Then our first son, Blake, was born. He was the new love of my life. I still liked having fun, but for me the scene was changing. As is so often the case with a first child, Blake had the effect of grounding me. His needs brought new purpose to my life. I had to think of him before making every decision. For Ron, however, the experience was different. Having a baby didn't really impact his thinking as much as it did mine. He was still working his day job and bringing home a paycheck, but he also continued to play in his band on the weekends. The more he was gone, the more isolated I felt.

If there was nothing worse in our story, this would be enough to put our marriage at risk. Most families who find themselves in this position do not survive. They end up estranged or divorced. We were like three people stuck on a rowboat miles out at sea. Precarious as it was, we had no idea that a storm was about to hit us.

In 1988, Brandon was born. We had moved to Utah to be near extended family and to pursue better work opportunities, but my secret hope was that the change in location would break some of the destructive patterns of behavior that had become entrenched in our still young family. Ron was trying hard to make things work. It was a strange time. Nothing was getting worse, but things were not getting any better either.

In the summer of 1988, Aaron, my relative, came to visit. Because both of Aaron's parents worked, he and I had always been close. I was like a second mother to him. When I left for college it was hard for him. When I married Ron, it was harder still. He seemed to resent my new husband, as though Ron had taken me away from him.

When I moved to Utah, Aaron was thirteen and having trouble in junior high school. He was experimenting with drugs and alcohol. His mother, "Martha," asked if he could stay with us in Utah for a few weeks during the summer. She was concerned that he would get in more trouble unless he had better supervision and a change of venue. The summer passed uneventfully and as the fall semester approached, Aaron returned home. After his return, however, things began to spiral out of control. The private school he attended decided that they were not equipped to work with him because he was addicted to drugs and alcohol. Treatments didn't seem to be working. After a year of struggling to help Aaron, his parents were concerned he would end up in prison, so they actively began looking for other alternatives to help him.

Utah was not what we had hoped for, so after about 2 years, Ron and I also decided to return to Ohio. The next year passed without incident as we were both going through the motions of family life, marriage, and work, each of us secretly wondering if our marriage was going to last.

Aaron's parents approached us to ask us if he could stay with us so he could attend a different school with a fresh start. I was willing, but Ron refused. Six weeks later, Aaron was sent away to a boys' home. (Although we were unaware, this institution was later investigated for practices of abuse and several staff members were eventually tried and convicted.)

It was while Aaron was at this home for boys that we were informed that Aaron had accused Ron of a horrible crime. There was no physical evidence that a crime had taken place. In fact, the only evidence for the accusation was based on an assisted resurrection of a repressed memory – a technique that has subsequently been disallowed in the evidentiary rules of the State of Ohio because it is notoriously faulty. Ron insisted that he was innocent and refused to accept a plea bargain of 6 months followed by release to probation. We went to trial. His court-appointed attorney, believing that the prosecutor had failed to present anything which would overcome the standard of maintaining reasonable doubt, decided that the best way to respond to the accusations at trial was to not offer a defense. All of Ron's witnesses were excused, and the defense rested his case.

Innocent but Found Guilty

Contrary to our attorney's opinion of how things would go for Ron, after asking the court to define "reasonable doubt" the jury found my husband guilty. At the sentencing, the judge said he doubted Ron's guilt, but was obliged under mandatory sentencing guidelines to sentence the accused. He pronounced that Ron Tijerina, who I absolutely knew was innocent, was now sentenced to 14 - 25 years in prison. To our disbelief, Ron was sent to a maximum security prison four hours away from our home. I cannot even begin to explain what those days were like for my small, young family.

The likelihood that a marriage will survive an incarceration is less than 30%. The likelihood that a marriage will survive reintegration from an extended incarceration is about 5%. I was exhausted from the court battles, wounded by Aaron's and his mother's testimony. I was ashamed of all of the negative publicity our case received in a small town, and I knew that the odds of survival were stacked against my family. The perfect storm had hit. Our rowboat, now with four members in the family, was capsized and we were clinging to anything just to survive.

The Solution

It's hard to believe that this was our life 22 years ago.

We were in a moment that comes, one way or another, to every life; the moment of utter failure. In this moment, it didn't matter that my relatives were actively working to destroy my marriage. It didn't matter that Ron was innocent. It didn't matter that the odds were stacked heavily against us. The only thing that mattered was what we were going to do with our circumstances; how were we going to respond?

I remember once watching a child who was trying to help his mother at the table. The child accidentally broke a piece of his mother's expensive china. The china had been her grandmother's, and she was grieved by the loss. But she paused for a moment, collected herself, calmly got down on the floor, and cleaned up the mess. She talked to her child as she carefully picked up each piece of the broken china. She encouraged him and assured him that he would be allowed to help in the future. It took five minutes, and then they moved on. They avoided all the bad endings that could have happened from that moment of sadness, and chose love and forgiveness instead. Having a healthy family does not come about by avoiding hurt and grief, but rather as a result of taking the effort to overcome those inevitable hurts.

The First Step – Own It!

Our lives were shattered. The life that we had formally known was gone forever. Even though we were grieving, and despite our immaturity and lack of closeness, the first thing we did was to acknowledge to each other that we alone were responsible for all of our actions and our decisions. To this day, I'm not entirely sure why it seemed like the only obvious response to our new circumstance. But I am so glad we did. It moved us out of being victimized and into a place of empowerment. We took ownership of all that we had done in those five short years of marriage; the good and the bad . . . every single thing in our lives that we had done or had left undone. We owned it. It was liberating, and, in some ways, it was the first moment of honesty and the start of our healing. It became the foundation on which we would together rebuild our life. We had nothing else; but it was all that we needed. We were carrying this heavy burden of unjust accusation; later, people would write of Ron's innocence and the miscarriage of justice, and the narrow window of opportunity that allowed this disaster to happen, but at that time, Ron was yet to be vindicated. What man used for evil, God amazingly used for good.

When a situation is this bad, nothing is easy; and yet, we made it through this process. We worked together to discover the principles of making a healthy family. We practiced these principles even when it felt impossible and especially when we didn't feel like doing it. This was, and remains, the most empowering experience that we have had in our entire lives. From this, we have formulated world-class curriculum for both families in acute crises as well as families who appear perfectly normal, but who also have underlying issues that need resolution and healing.

Using the High Five – The Story of Dave and Tina

We met "Dave" about four years ago. He and his wife "Tina" were on the verge of separating. She was hurt, scared and felt isolated and uncared for by her husband. Dave was cocky, arrogant, and completely self-centered, though he didn't have much to be proud of: He was in prison for manufacturing drugs out of his house. Dave and Tina had two small children, one of them an infant. Dave's lifestyle put his family's life in jeopardy, and now it had taken him away from them, leaving them with no income, no husband, no father, and no protection.

Though separated physically, Dave didn't want to lose his wife, but he attempted to control Tina by belittling her and undermining her confidence. Tina began to believe his negativity and lies; their marriage was on the verge of breaking under the weight of their circumstances combined with Dave's abusive control. Dave feared that something was wrong, and he could feel his family slipping away from him. It was at this vulnerable time that Dave heard about our program. When he talked about it with Tina, she encouraged him to sign up. He did, thinking that at the very least, he might be able to see Tina more often if she participated.

Neither Dave nor Tina knew what they were in for. Once in the program, as we explained the principles that make a family strong and healthy, Dave stopped trying to control his family. Amazingly, he began encouraging his wife; it was thrilling to watch him do everything that he could to support her from a distance. Tina learned how to navigate through the hurts and pains to forgive Dave, and together they learned how to trust one another again.

Today, Dave is no longer in prison; he is home with his family. He is active in his community and his church and has been promoted several times by his employer. Tina is loved, supported, and protected. She feels liberated. Their children are succeeding in school, and their family couldn't be happier. Dave and Tina could have settled for something else. If they called it quits or just got tired of the continual work, no one would have blamed them for failing in the midst of their poor patterns and the separation caused by prison. But, instead they chose to apply the High Five in their life. It changed them forever!

Cathy - The Perfect Couple...?

The restaurant was buzzing with Wednesday evening chatter. People all around us were greeting friends and talking about the day's work. Opposite Ron and I was a well-dressed, seemingly successful couple. This was our first meeting to discuss the possibility of him working with The RIDGE Project. They were both at ease with business dining, and we made our way through the ice-breaking of polite conversation prior to ordering. Once the server had left with our order, we began talking in more detail.

Although the husband was relatively young, he described how he had become successful early in life and had made a great deal of money. They both described the pleasure each took in parenting their children. Now, he said, he wanted to give back to those less fortunate by working in one of our organizations.

This in itself is actually very common. We're consistently amazed by

the extraordinarily successful people who approach us either to make financial contributions or to work as volunteers in retirement. But as the man was speaking, Ron briefly glanced my way with an expression that let me know he detected something wasn't right. I had the same feeling.

Nothing was obviously wrong. The story that they told about their life together was entirely plausible; but their body language and the lack of referencing one another in conversation was hard for me to reconcile in my mind. I was wondering what was going on when Ron simply asked the couple to tell us about the greatest struggle in their relationship and how they had overcome it.

The couple paused. It was that look that a child gets when he is caught with his hand in the cookie jar. There was nowhere to hide. They looked at each other for a moment, and then the husband slowly began to tell their story. He confessed that their marriage was a sham. Though they had retained their marital status, they had not lived together for several years. They were both involved in romantic relationships with other people and they kept the relationship going primarily for social reasons.

On the surface, the couple looked so polished. They had their routine down. And the husband in particular was so earnest in genuinely wanting to help others. It was heart-wrenching and it would have been shocking if it was the first time we had heard this story, but one of the things that we've learned over the last 22 years is that it doesn't matter where families come from or what the individual members of those families may have accomplished – a healthy family doesn't just happen.

Ron gently told the husband that he could not join our organization, even as a volunteer, under the present circumstances because he did not have the thing that people need most. He did not have a healthy family. He needed to learn those principles before he could hope to help anyone else. Over the next three hours, Ron and I were able to explain the High Five, share our story with them, and give them the tools to build

24

a healthy family. As we shared together, they told us how they had met and what they had hoped for when they married. They described the drift that set in as they worked long hours in different worlds. It was emotional. We shared their stories of pain and their memories of joy with both tears and laughter. And we challenged them that maybe their story was not yet over. It was a small but joyful surprises when, the next day, Ron received a telephone call from the man. On the drive home the man and his wife decided to try again and he asked to be able to call in the future if they needed more counsel.

There is Another Way!

Many families have settled for living in the chaos of broken and distant relationships. It is a tragedy to see so many living second-class lives. No matter how wonderful a family may look from the outside, too many have settled for unfulfilling relationships and unhealthy lifestyles. Sadly, they don't believe they can have something better. They don't have the skills to make their family relationships thriving, healthy, and vibrant. The High Five principles can transform families from suffering to successful. If these concepts worked for us with our unimaginable challenges, they can work for anyone.

Fight Each Other… or Fight FOR Each Other?

Nobody starts something hoping to fail. The older couple at the market didn't choose to marry hoping for the bitterness that seeped into their lives over the years. The mother didn't choose to raise her daughter hoping that one day, while buying a cell phone, she would be the cause of pain and suffering. I didn't marry Ron with any intention of visiting him behind bars before our sixth anniversary, but sometimes we don't live the dream we start out envisioning. In reality, none of us is immune from life's challenges. And, because there's no vaccine to protect against unhealthy families, we have to work out our problems the hard way. If we want a strong and healthy family, we need to fight for it.

I cannot imagine throwing fists at someone or belittling my spouse in public. Ron and I refuse to allow that to happen in our marriage. Instead, we are intentionally fighting to build success and to support each other. In this book we share with you the secrets we have learned; secrets to build your family up and keep it intact no matter what your circumstances are. The High Five will transform your family from the ordinary to the exceptional. No matter what your condition or your

circumstances, if you apply these principles, you will have success. Just like with Betty Crocker, if you follow the recipe, you will have good results in the end; a stronger, more dedicated family that can overcome any obstacle.

FRIENDSHIP

FAITHFULNESS

FORGIVENESS

FAIRNESS

FORTITUDE

Chapter 3

Ron and Bria – Learning to Do the Job the Right Way

A few years ago we bought our daughter, Bria, a quarter-pony. One day Bria and I were at the stable, cleaning and tending to the horse. I wasn't raised around horses so I watched as she cleaned the horse's hooves. As she worked, I asked if she would show me how to clean them. She immediately began to give me a lesson on how to care for a horse. As she was picking the dirt out the hoof, she explained that I should always clean the horse hooves with the hook going away; "Never, ever pull it toward you, Papa," she told me very seriously. "Of course," I said. "But Bria, why can't I pull it toward me?" I asked, thinking that the reason was that I could gouge out my eye with the hoof pick. She said, "Because if you go towards your face, the mud and horse poo will fly in your face, silly!"

It is important to have the right tools for the job and to know how to use them properly.

A Healthy Family Doesn't Just Happen

We live in a world where most people express an interest in being healthy. In fact, I am convinced that if someone took a poll, most people would say that they would like to have more energy, greater physical stamina, better mental clarity and greater resistance to disease. It comes as no surprise that the world is filled with different diet and exercise strategies to help people accomplish these goals. Here's an interesting observation; most diet and exercise programs work if they are followed. It may be that some work better than others or that some people are better suited for one kind of approach to health than they are to another. But people who take seriously the program they have chosen as their path to physical well-being usually get what they are trying for.

When someone really determines in their mind that they are going to achieve a higher state of physical health, they will become healthier.

Sometimes this determination comes as a result of disease; a cancer scare or heart attack can get almost anyone motivated to improve their health. Occasionally, it comes from knowing someone who is deeply committed to healthy living and recognizing the vibrancy of their life and the freedom they enjoy from stress and disease.

It's the same with a healthy family. We know of one couple who, upon becoming engaged, made a list of long-married couples and made a point of visiting each one in order to ask them the reason for their success. This young couple recognized what they wanted and began to practice the habits that were likely to bring them the result they desired. Unfortunately, more families approach us for coaching or attend a seminar only after their family relationships are deeply scarred with unhealthy patterns of behavior. It's not that even deeply injured families can't be healed; the misfortune is the unnecessary pain and suffering.

Bodily health and healthy families have one other important parallel. There is no one who has a perfect body. It's not even an appropriate way to think about bodily health. No one who exercises regularly believes that they are going to one day be perfect. In the same way, nobody who spends time and effort working toward having a healthy family believes that someday they will attain a perfect relationship.

Any physical trainer worth their salt will tell you that there is no such thing as a perfect body. Life doesn't work this way. There is, however, such a thing as a healthy body – a body that can give you the freedom to be mobile, the energy to achieve, and perhaps most importantly, a body that can resist disease. In the same way, there is no such thing as a perfect family, but there are healthy families. A healthy family liberates and empowers the people in the family. Perhaps most importantly, it is a means to build the necessary resistance that will prevent disease from creeping into the most important and fulfilling relationships of your life.

What is considered "normal" is constantly changing and families are being challenged in new ways every day. Demanding work schedules, media, music, fashion, and the internet are all influencing families' values and norms. As families struggle to adapt to the new definition of a normal family, society continues to redefine normal for each member of the family individually. Self-centeredness slowly fragments families, destroying families from within and making them even more vulnerable to attacks from outside forces. This problem is not isolated to any demographic; family breakdown does not discriminate based upon race, social status or geography. No family is unaffected by the trials that tear families apart. Healthy families know how to navigate through those trials to become healthier and stronger.

More marriages are failing, and more children are turning to destructive behaviors as a result of the rapid disintegration of the family. Strong families, what used to be the cornerstone of success in life and business, are now referred to as the "fairy tale." Increasing numbers of families are accepting dysfunctional and dissatisfying relationships as inevitable. Out of this rubble of broken families emerge men and women who are "looking for love in all the wrong places" with no idea how to build and maintain a strong and healthy family.

We Refused to Give Up

Our family refused to submit to the statistics or accept that our marriage and family were doomed to fail. We determined to build the strongest foundation possible for our children. Since giving up on our family was unimaginable, we did all we could to change the landscape for our future while still in the midst of the unimaginable. We adopted the "never give up" attitude toward our marriage and family. It didn't erase the obstacles; it empowered us to overcome.

The goal is not to be just like us. No set of relationships are exactly alike. Each marriage and family is a unique blend of the people and personalities that make up that unit. This difference and uniqueness is what makes every family exciting and alive. We can, and should, emulate the healthy habits of other couples, but we can never be just like any other couple because our relationship is unique. So many times, couples get caught up trying so hard to be just like the couple they know that appears to be "perfect" instead of building upon their own unique strengths and personalities. This pretense leaves them feeling even more empty and frustrated. Joe and Linda can never be Ron and Cathy. But Joe and Linda can develop their family into a healthy, thriving family and experience a deeply satisfying relationship of their own!

Achieving Family Fitness

Practicing the High Five principles of a successful, healthy family are very much like a program of physical exercises. When people are serious about physical health they typically enter into a program of diet and exercise. They begin eating better foods and limit or omit other kinds of foods. They exercise with weights for strength and do aerobic exercise to develop endurance. And in each area, the more they practice and develop their skills, the better they become. When a person runs on a regular basis, they develop the ability to run further and faster. When a person lifts weights, they become stronger and can increase the amount of weight or resistance. As a person begins to associate what they eat with an increased energy level and feeling of well-being, they start choosing foods that will actually bring them into an optimal state of energy and alertness and reject those foods that cause them to feel sluggish and tired.

Succeeding in Your Family Fitness Program

In order to achieve success, you need to have goals and stay committed. Knowing what to do is a matter of training. Being committed is a measure of how much you want success. This is the path to a healthy family as well as the path to a healthy body. When you want to have success, it is important to know how to achieve your goals. Learning the High Five will help you learn the right way to have a strong, happy family.

Strong family Relationships are Key to Personal Success – Friendship is born out of the most basic social need, which is to share. Sharing is one of the most natural of all human instincts. We all desire the security of sharing our most intimate or creative thoughts, hoping to find honest affirmation and personal acceptance, without fear of rejection – just freedom to share. Friendship is a gift. No other gift is more welcome or more readily received. The amazing thing about friendship is that you have the power to give that gift to anyone at any time. The more you do and the longer you live in friendship, the stronger you will become. As the depth and importance of your friendships increase, so does your success. Remember: "If you want to have a friend, then be a friend."

Learn what it means to be truly faithful. Usually when people use this word they are talking about fidelity to their marriage vows. It makes us sad that anyone settles for such a

> "Without faithfulness, friendship is impossible."

limited and impoverished understanding of the true meaning of faithfulness. Faithfulness is about bringing honor to another person and never doing anything which would dishonor them or their good name. Without faithfulness, friendship is impossible. Faithfulness is the foundation that allows one person to trust another. When it is present, it frees all of a person's relationships to thrive openly and honestly. Anyone who learns the deepest meaning of faithfulness and practices it will be surrounded by friends. In fact, friendship with other members of your family is the evidence that you are a faithful person – and evidence that you are developing a healthy family.

Forgive others. It is a strange paradox that we all fail others and offend or let them down, and then have a hard time forgiving other people when they fail us. Because it is inevitable that others are going to fail us, learning to forgive is an essential High Five principle necessary for successful and empowering relationships. On the other hand, the failure to forgive makes it impossible to have successful, stable, long-term relationships. Practicing forgiveness is like getting ready to do a set of your least favorite exercises. However, forgiving others consistently and completely is crucial in order to keep friendships alive.

Activate fairness in your relationships. Fairness is not about whether or not we have been treated fairly. It is the commitment to live by a certain set of rules. We all seem to be acutely aware of those moments when we have not been treated fairly by a family member, but we often do not recognize our own selfish behaviors. It is possible to learn to manage our expectations, to stay committed to following the rules that show fairness to others, and to examine our own motives to help us consider others before acting.

Develop the fortitude needed to overcome every obstacle. Fortitude is different from all the other High Five principles mentioned. In achieving family health, the other principles are like performing exercises, but fortitude is more like following a diet. It is the practice of choosing those things that are excellent and rejecting those that are inferior, valuing the things which are essential for a healthy family and pursuing it with your whole heart. It is about doing what is right and refusing to compromise because in this diet, you really are what you eat.

Ron – Pride and the Jet Ski

The sun was high in the bright blue sky; the sand on the beach was hot against our bare feet as we ran into the cool water together. My daughter's excitement was contagious. As she rushed toward the Jet Ski I found myself running past her to get there first. I lifted her up, out of the water and onto our water chariot and checked the clips on her lifejacket to be sure they were securely fastened. I disconnected the vehicle from the dock, pushing it away so I could safely start the engine.

"Ron, did you check the gas?" Cathy asked as she and our grandchildren made their way across the sand to see us off. "No, I am sure it is fine." I reassured her. I put the safety key in the compartment and started the motor.

Bria giggled out loud as we began our journey out on the lake. It was the perfect father and daughter activity! I sped up and began our trip around the lake. Bria was laughing and screaming at the same time as I did figure eights and serpentine patterns in the lake. I found myself laughing with her and enjoying the moment even more than I had antic- ipated. I came up on the turn to begin our journey back to the cottage dock when the Jet Ski began to sputter and then suddenly stopped. I tried to restart the engine over and over again. I looked around and saw several other boaters near us. Bria, who was increasingly concerned that she was going to be stuck out here in the middle of the lake, re- minded me that we had a safety whistle. "Blow the whistle, Papa!" she urged, "someone will hear it and come to help us."

I looked down at the whistle. There was no way I was going to blow that whistle! "No, Bria. I am not going to blow the whistle. That whistle is for real emergencies. This is not an emergency. We are just out of gas."

I looked across the lake and could make out my destination around the next bend. "See, right over there is where we are going." I tried to reas- sure her. "Papa! That is too far. I can't swim that far. Blow the whistle and someone will come help us," she pleaded. But I was adamant; I was not going to further embarrass myself by asking for help. I would just pull the Jet Ski across the lake, I decided.

I jumped off the side, grabbed the rope and began to swim. Wow! That Jet Ski was much heavier than I thought it would be as I pulled it behind me while I worked to swim across the lake. I swam. I rested. I swam and rested again. Bria had relaxed and was lying across the seat enjoying the ride home. It was getting more and more difficult to swim and pull Bria's newfound chaise lounge behind me.

I had only made it half way back, and I wasn't sure I could swim any lon- ger. My arms were tired, I was out of breath. I needed to take another break. Bria must have sensed I was losing this battle because she began to frantically wave her arms. I decided it was time to blow the whistle. "OK, Bria, go ahead and blow the whistle." I said before I climbed back onto the Jet Ski.

Bria blew the whistle long and loud. I looked up and saw Cathy stand- ing on the dock. I began to wave to her, hoping she was getting my

message. "Come and get us." I said. I could see her putting our two grandchildren in the row boat and rowing slowly over to us. As they got closer, I could hear my 2 year old grandson yelling, "We're coming Paw-paw; we will save you!"

I had to laugh. I was flooded with relief as Cathy pulled up next to us. We tied the rope from the Jet Ski to the rowboat. Cathy and I rowed back to the dock laughing softly about my adventure. As we made our way out of the boat, Cathy asked me if I had checked the reserve tank.

"Reserve tank? This thing has a reserve tank?" I checked it and sure enough, it was full. I was so humiliated! I had nearly drowned myself in pride pulling a Jet Ski with a reserve tank full of gas. My concern over what others would think had kept me from blowing the whistle and getting help as soon as I realized something was wrong. Had I called for help right away, someone would have come, checked my reserve tank, and I could have avoided the unnecessary struggles I had just endured. I vowed to never make that mistake again. When I need help, I ask for it.

Pride and fear are our worst enemies when it comes to getting help. Fear of what people will think about us, or about our circumstances, tricks us into keeping up the pretense of a perfect relationship. Asking for help would require us to destroy the illusion of perfection; we would be admitting we don't have all the answers, that we need assistance. Pride will keep us stuck in our own "stuckness" – trapped in a place we don't even want to be.

Challenges You Will Face

As soon as you commit to using the High Five and helping your family to grow and become healthy, you will experience more resistance and opposition. One of these is purely psychological. We call this the "mind battle." When you start to actively pursue improved health for your family, you may find the voice of doubt creeping into your mind and filling you with fearful questions. "Is this really possible?" "Is it worth the effort?" We hear these questions from clients all the time.

Another common challenge is not having other family members on board. One of the greatest challenges in life is overcoming the feeling of being physically or socially isolated or alone. When one person in a family embraces the vision of a loving, healthy family but others in the family remain unconvinced, it can be very discouraging. Clients tell us, "I'm the only one trying" or "I'm the only one who really wants this." It is hard enough to drag yourself to the gym, but when you have to drag your spouse and unwilling children with you, it can feel nearly impossible.

The most difficult challenges often come from outside the immediate family. No matter what change you hope to make in your life, if you've got a goal then there is sure to be someone, usually not very far away, who will tell you that what you want is impossible. Even amongst our own families and closest friends, there can be enemies of our success. They will go to great lengths to explain to you why this won't work for you.

As you begin to pursue your dreams, these people are the first ones to point out why it won't work, what is going to go wrong, and how ridiculous you are for thinking otherwise. These discouragers are stuck in the fear of other peoples' opinions or the fear of failure. Do not allow them to keep you from pursuing success for your family. Remember, the example of your success can inspire others to eventually break poor habits, overcome their fear and find their victory.

It is important to understand that all changes are accompanied by challenges. When you work to make a situation better in your life and have success, then it leaves others without anything to say. The part of the equation that we often fail to understand is that when we work and we succeed, it puts pressure on other people and makes them feel that they must also work to improve. Nobody wants pressure, so their response is to discourage us from attempting and succeeding so they can take that pressure off of themselves. They may appear to be trying to help, saying things like, "I just don't want to see you get hurt," or, "Are things really so bad that you have to make changes?" or, "This doesn't really work." But the hurt is already there; unless things change, the hurt won't go away.

You can't lead where you won't go, so if you are intent on leading your family with the High Fives, you must practice these principles yourself and ignore the opinions of the discouragers who are waiting to derail your dreams, again. Initially, change itself can appear to be worse than the pain of the current situation. Fear of change can be the most paralyzing obstacle of all. Not everyone is afraid of change, but if you are, it can immobilize you. The truth, though, is that life is change. We are always changing – our bodies, our minds, our relationships. We are constantly in motion; like the rotation of the earth, it can be hard to see it, but it is true. There are only two directions that we can go in life; we can grow and change for the better, or refuse to grow and change for the worse. There is no standing still; change is inevitable, but we can decide how change will be implemented in our lives.

You Can Overcome the Obstacles in Your Path!

You can develop the strategies to overcome every obstacle you will experience on the path to having a healthy family. Every problem has a solution to it; the hardest part is remembering to look for that solution. Once you identify the right solution, it is simple. But being simple is not the same thing as being easy, and achieving the solution requires determination. When you commit to being successful, you prepare yourself to face the obstacles in your path and develop the tools necessary to overcome them and achieve success. If you realize that success only comes from the process of facing challenges, that knowledge can help you be prepared to tackle them with energy and creativity.

Practice doesn't make perfect, but it does make permanent. Practicing these techniques will make you strong enough to overcome the obstacles and give you success. Just like diet and exercise, if you do the work, you will achieve results, and the health of your family will improve. In the world of diet and exercise, sometimes people don't practice enough to get the

"Practice makes permanent"

results that they want. I have a friend who owns a gym, and she says that the gym is always full on January second, but there are only a few cars in the lot by the fourth of July.

How to Overcome

The way to overcome these obstacles is twofold. First, you have to surround yourself with positive messages that affirm that a healthy family is possible for you and your family. Reading this book and getting connected to some of our other family support opportunities is a great place to start!

Secondly, learn and practice the skills you need to make that dream a reality. If you don't know what things you need to do, or what skills you need to practice, then keep reading. But don't stop there! Believe it or not, there is a whole emerging industry devoting itself to encouraging families to enter into the reality of having a healthy family. Over the last twenty years we have seen many other people and organizations that are doing quality work helping with parenting and developing vibrant marriages. When you work out in a gym where people take their fitness seriously, it helps you to become part of a movement. The message of hope will seem more achievable every day.

While these are universal principles that will work for every family and couple, they also allow your individuality as a couple to flourish. You will have the opportunity to find the beauty of the unique characteristics of your own family and who you are together and unwrap that gift every day. By applying the High Five in your family, you will also define what is acceptable and healthy in your own relationship. What a wonderful adventure! As you navigate through each of these chapters and read our stories, our hope is that you will see how they relate to your struggles and that you will perceive echoes of your family in our family's journey.

Building a strong and healthy marriage and family requires a significant amount of courage. You must have the courage to acquire and then apply the skills and information that help you grow stronger, but you must also find the courage to be different and unique. We stopped trying to be normal a long time ago! We have embraced the fact that we are not average or normal. We are Ron and Cathy and our children are genetically linked to us. The "us" in this relationship is so unique and so exciting to explore because there is not any other couple or family just like us.

The High Five

Without Friendship, Faithfulness, Forgiveness, Fairness, and Fortitude, families can never experience the joy that comes from a deep, connected bond that can be forged through hardship and adversity. The High Five principles will take you and your family to a whole new level in your relationships. These skills will stabilize your family and deepen your relationships. As you begin your journey toward deeper and more fulfilling relationships, you will find that the concepts move you into a place of peace and joy even in the midst of difficult circumstances. The High Five are waiting to transform your life. It is time to experience health in your family and the high that comes with success!

Friendship: Building lasting bonds through fun and laughter; sharing of life's struggles and victories while committing to be loyal.

Ron – What Friendship is Made Of

In prison, you get the opportunity to talk with people from many different cultures. One of the things I have observed is that there is a common thread running through religions and faiths: the importance of sharing. The Japanese tea ceremony is about sharing an experience. The feasts of the early Christian church are about sharing. The Jewish Day of Atonement is about sharing the celebration of being released from failings. Sharing experiences is what creates friendship.

Friendship is a word you do not throw around or take lightly in prison. There is always a feeling in the air of distrust no matter how well you think you know another person, even if you have been sharing meals together for more than 10 years. You want to believe the best of people, but when you are in prison, you cannot help but wonder whether someone is a true friend or not. And yet, all of us longed for real friendship, even though many of us wouldn't have even know how to define it.

Since those days, I have learned that true friendship takes tenacity. It is not something that happens overnight. It is a long process, and it can be full of trials and tribulations. A true friendship is something that is fought for and earned. True friendship is genuine, unconditional love; it is valuing the good in someone as well as forgiving the bad. The committed love between husband and wife is a beautiful picture of true friendship. But it can be hard to find, and once formed, friendship needs continued nurturing if it is to grow strong. I met a lot of people in the 15 years I was in prison, but sadly, I can count only a few as friends I would have at my house.

Ron - Selfishness is the Enemy of Friendship

One of the best kept secrets to maintaining a healthy and sustainable friendship is to not take anything personally. Forgiving the offenses that come from another person is difficult, but it's what makes maintaining a strong friendship that can handle the test of time possible. I believe the leading cause of divorce in American today is NOT money, religion, or even unfaithfulness; these are just symptoms. The real sickness that attacks the hope of having a successful family is selfishness. Selfishness, in my opinion, is the leading cause of many evils that plague the world today. When we focus on "me," then we lose sight of "us." When the selfishness of a father causes him to value other things more highly than his family, whether it is his work, his friends, or the embrace of another woman, he is not a father at all. He is just a child still playing house, not a man building one.

Cathy – Teaching Sharing and Friendship to Dawson

I remember when our grandson, Dawson, was 2 years old, and Ron taught him the joy that comes from sharing with a friend. Ron had been home from prison for four wonderful years, and our oldest son, Blake, was married and had a son.

It happened to be one of those really beautiful fall days; the kind that makes you think summer changed her mind and decided to return. The sun shone bright and coaxed the crisp air warmer by the hour. The light breeze moved gently across the leaves in the trees causing them to dance with delight. But those things paled in comparison to the sight of 2-year-old Dawson. Dawson is a sweet-faced little red-haired boy. He was running back and forth across the yard chasing bubbles. His Grandpa, Ron, was sitting on the edge of the deck, blowing bubbles that floated in the air all around his beloved grandson. Dawson ran squealing, chasing the bubbles and popping as many as he could touch. His sparkling blue eyes were full of excitement, and bits of grass were stuck in his bright red hair as evidence of his numerous tumbles. He smiled and laughed while he bounded around the yard on his quest to pop all the bubbles he could before anyone else could reach them. This was the kind of day we had longed for all those years that Ron was in prison.

I had a plate of freshly baked chocolate chip cookies for the guys, but I was reluctant to interrupt this precious moment. Just then, Ron saw me with the cookies and announced it was time to take a break to eat a warm chocolate chip cookie. Dawson abandoned his bubble hunt and darted over to grab a cookie. "Mine coo-key!" he announced as he ran off with one of the cookies. He found a small stool on the deck and plopped down on it, swinging his short legs back and forth while thoroughly enjoying his cookie. Ron and I glanced at each other to make sure neither of us missed watching him bite into the gooey cookie and lick his fingers, getting melted chocolate all over his round little face. He ran back up to his Grandpa and demanded another cookie. Ron broke a small piece of his own cookie and handed it to Dawson. Dawson popped it in his mouth and then reached for another piece from Ron's cookie. "Dawson, this is my cookie," Ron explained to him, "but I will share it with you."

> When we focus on "me," then we lose sight of "us."

Ron offered his cookie to Dawson. "Do you want a bite, Dawson?" Dawson opened his mouth wide and took a big bite. A little too big! Part of the cookie stayed in his mouth and the rest came back out . . . soggy. "OK, Dawson, you can have it," Ron conceded after evaluating the current state of his cookie. Dawson took the cookie and examined it. "Paw-paw bite?" he asked as he offered it to his Grandpa. Surprised, Ron quickly responded, "Yes, thank you, Dawson, I would love to share that cookie with you!" Dawson gently, and with a deliberate look on his face, put a piece of the cookie into Ron's mouth. Dawson watched Ron chew it; then he looked down at the piece of cookie left in his hand and a smile spread across his face. His eyes lit up! His delight was evident as he announced, "Maw-maw, I share!" He turned back to Ron and offered him another bite, and another one until the cookie was gone. He grabbed another cookie and began feeding it to his grandpa. He would take a bite and then offer it to Ron. His bites were small and careful as he shared his treat. His face glowed with his new-found joy: friendship.

He had just discovered that the experience of sharing something with someone he loved was so much better than eating a cookie all alone.

Ron – Sharing is the Glue of Family Life

It is a beautiful moment when we realize that the gift of sharing our lives with someone else is better than experiencing things alone. This is the foundation of friendship. In a single moment, Dawson realized that he had the power to bring pleasure to someone else by sharing something that he himself enjoyed. The joy of giving something to me, his grandfather, was even greater than the immediate pleasure of eating the cookie himself. What a powerful thing to observe. Even in the innocence, or perhaps especially in the innocence of a small child, we find the great good of sharing. At its core, this is the glue of family. The pleasure of shared experiences, the better understanding of yourself that comes from sharing ourselves with another, and the meaning that comes from living out a shared story – these things build a foundation that make possible an empowered life of success and achievement.

In 1991, when I was first incarcerated, I was sent to the Corrections Reception Center (CRC), where they assess new prisoners and assign them to a prison to serve their time. That was the time I began to really examine my life and see what it truly was. I hated what I saw. I had acted like a selfish little boy who believed in nothing but a lie. Growing up in a family of musicians I bought into the fantasy that I was a superstar. I thought that because I could play the drums and could make people happy with my music, I was both irresistible and invincible. I believed that I did not have to work, that my music and my charm would pay my bills and get me whatever I wanted. Foolishly, I lived my life believing my ability to play music would solve all my problems. Everywhere I went, people liked me and were attracted to me because I was talented; at least that is what I told myself. Little did I know it was just a figment of my imagination. In truth I was a loser, or in prison terms, a "lame" – the lowest of the low. Looking back and seeing the guy that I was makes me rejoice that he no longer exists.

I believe that every man has something in his life that is his Achilles' heel. If we do not constantly work on it, we will walk with a limp and become so used to it; we may not even be conscious of it. My Achilles heel was my own ego. I believed I could do whatever I wanted to do, and there would be no consequences. If I wanted to stay out all night, I did. If I wanted to get drunk or high, I did. I thoroughly enjoyed all the attention I received as the drummer in a band. I loved the way the fans would stare at me, scream for me, and blush when I flashed my smile at them. I felt important and unconquerable. At first, I would just flirt and lead girls on… then dash their hopes by showing them my wedding ring. But then, the flirting became the desire to pursue another woman. My thoughts were preoccupied with finding an opportunity to pursue and win over this new woman in my life. My beautiful wife was unaware of the internal battle I had just lost. I had purposed in my heart to be unfaithful to her.

Brandon – Friendship is About Sharing Experiences that Sometimes are Not Very Fun

It is true. Creating and maintaining a friendship is work; sometimes it is a lot of work. It involves giving time and energy. But when you see the relationship as something that has a high value, then the work needed to maintain the friendship takes on a new dimension. As you practice building your friendships, the effort seems more natural and less like work. It is still a choice you make though; it still involves effort. But it's not the drudgery that we sometimes associate with "work."

I can't tell you how often my friends have helped me get through situations that at the time seemed impossible. Because my circumstances growing up created some unusual challenges, I feel especially blessed to have true friends; we have been through so much together. One of the best things about having long and trusted friendships is the knowledge that, no matter what type of situation I am in, I can call them and they will come help me get through it. Last winter, as I was driving home one dark Ohio night, my truck tire blew out. I called one of my friends to help me change it and he immediately stopped what he was doing and came to help me. It was freezing outside, and our hands were hurting because we were so cold so we both were complaining, but he stayed and helped me till the job was done. On one level I am sure he was thinking, "Why didn't I just let that phone call go to voice mail?!" But now it is a moment of bonding that we share in our memories. Whenever I see him, he asks me if I have checked my tires recently. We both smile, remembering the difficult moment of adversity that we shared. It has become a special bond in our friendship.

Another time, one of my friends had just washed his trailer and then was driving it around to air dry it on a country road (well … we DO live in rural Ohio!). The trailer wasn't fastened securely, and it fell off the hitch. He called me and asked if I could come help him to get the trailer back on the hitch, so I stopped what I was doing and came to his rescue. Now when I see him I ask if he's "properly hitched!" We shared a small moment of adversity, and that strengthened our friendship. Sometimes you have to choose to do unexciting or just plain unpleasant things to help your friends. But it strengthens friendships in a way that nothing else can. If you embrace that, your life will be filled with a special joy and a deep sense of meaning.

Ron – Friendship Requires Honest Communication

Unfaithfulness is a symptom of brokenness in a man. It is not the glorious act so many men think it is, or imagine that it will be. It is chasing after elusive self-fulfillment that ends with a self-inflicted mortal wound. Adultery is an act of suicide that kills the heart of honor and poisons everything it breathes upon. It is born out of brokenness and breeds even more deceit, lust and destruction. If only I had known or had been even slightly conscious that my careless action would lead to years of pain and regret, I can say with certainty I would not have done it. I had no idea what a high price I would pay because of my ignorance.

When I first went to prison I began to read the Bible, and I remember reading a passage (Proverbs 7) for the first time. This passage describes a young man who abandons everything that he knows is right and good in order to engage in adultery. Wow! It scared me so much that it took me a few weeks to get brave enough to read my Bible again. Seeing my reflection in this book frightened me. To see the truth stated with so much boldness took me by surprise. I was the young man being written about; someone going to a place where they had no business being. I was a fool and allowed my selfish desires to feed the lie that I would not get burned by this act of betrayal. I told myself that no one would ever know.

It still is difficult for me to say the words, let alone put it down on paper, but here it goes. I was unfaithful to my wife. I had affairs with other women and I betrayed my marriage vows to my wife, Cathy.

> "Unfaithfulness is a symptom of brokenness in a man."

It was in 1991 when I found enough courage to tell her the truth. I was behind bars, but in my heart and my mind, I was starting to be set free. In the first five years of our marriage, she had asked me from time to time if I ever went out on her. I would tell her, "No, sweetheart. I love you." But the problem was that I didn't know what real love was. My idea of love was an illusion; one that was centered on me and my own selfish view of what love really meant. In my mind, since I never thought I had stopped loving her, I had never really cheated on her. I had only had sex with someone else. I was thinking that love was only a feeling and not related to my selfish actions.

Something strange was beginning to happen. After sitting in prison for a few months, I began to change into the man that I wish I had been from the beginning. I was changing into a man who was worth following, one who knew who he was and did not need to convince himself of his value by pursuing other women. One day while Cathy and I were talking on the phone, Cathy asked me the big question again. "When you were in Utah and the boys and I moved back to Ohio before you did, did you go out on me? Were you unfaithful?" In that moment, I knew that this new man I was becoming could not run anymore. I knew

I had to be completely honest with her so we could survive this new, difficult chapter in our lives with the right foundation.

I was afraid of what her response might be. I knew that if I told her the truth, she might hang up that phone and she and my two sons – the most important people in my life – would walk away forever. As all of these fears swirled about in my mind, I knew that if we were going to make it through this season of our marriage, we had to build it right, and some of the bricks had to be openness and honesty. So I told Cathy the truth. "Yes," I said softly, "I had an affair." I braced myself for the hail of words and anger that I knew I deserved. I never expected the response I received. Cathy's voice was completely calm. She said, "I know. I have known for a long time." She then asked me if it was hard to admit it. "No it wasn't, not anymore, but I am afraid of losing you," I confessed. I then told Cathy how very sorry I was. After that, she asked me if there had been anyone else. I then told her of another woman who had been a friend of ours. I couldn't tell her enough how very sorry I was.

I could hear the hurt, pain, and disappointment in her voice. It was so tangible I could feel her heart breaking. I had robbed her of something she could never get back; a husband who kept his wedding vow to her. It is a feeling I never, ever want to experience again, and I decided within myself that I never would.

Cathy – Rebuilding Marriage on a New Foundation

I really do not know what caused me to ask Ron if he had been unfaithful to me in the early years of our marriage. I suspected that he had had an affair, but I had never had anything more concrete than a sense of knowing in my heart that he had been with another woman. Even as I asked the question, I had a sense that this time his answer would be different. As much as I had longed to know the truth, his next words still came as a shock to me. "Yes." Yes? Yes?! No!! The right answer, the answer my heart longed to hear was, "NO." "But you knew intuitively that he had been unfaithful," I chided myself.

Pain ripped through my being and settled in my stomach. I fought the urge to throw up while I calmly told him that I had known the answer in my heart for a long time. I wished that the "knowing" could block the pain of the betrayal. I asked the next difficult question. "Who else?" I longed for him to say that there had not been anyone else. As he proceeded to tell me the truth about his unfaithfulness, I struggled to hold my composure. The words "How could he? How could she? Why?" whirled through my head in a vicious chase. The phone attendant announced that we had 30 seconds left on the call. Ron shared his final apology and promises for a future filled with love, honor and faithfulness before the phone went dead.

I stood in the hall of my friend's home with the receiver against my ear for another full minute. I knew that once I hung up that phone, I would have to begin to deal with all the emotions that were racing through me and begin to process the information I had just received. I hung up the phone and stared at the floor for a few more moments before collecting my wits about me. I quickly thanked my friend for allowing me to use her phone while I gathered up my precious sons and ushered them out to my car. I strapped them into their seats and climbed behind the wheel. As I pulled out of her driveway onto the street, the tears rolled down my cheeks unchecked. I silently wept while I drove the 20 minutes back to our trailer.

I drove past the miles of tasseled corn stalks, past the hog farm only ½ mile from my home, and pulled into the drive in front of the trailer we rented as our home. I switched the car off and glanced back at my sons. They were both sound asleep, to my immense relief. I bowed my head against the cold steering wheel as the tears poured down my face. After a while, I looked up. I caught a glimpse of my reflection in the rearview mirror. "Why is everything in your life such a mess?" I asked the girl with the swollen red eyes who looked defiantly back at me in the mirror. I pushed myself back in my seat and stared out the window. How on earth did I land here? Twenty-four years old, on welfare, living in this trailer in the middle of nowhere, married to a man who cheated on me and is in prison for the next 14-25 years for something he didn't do!

My life sounded like a badly written soap opera! But it wasn't a made-up story; it was my current reality. I lacked the will to move even one step forward. I looked up at the roof of my home and saw the tires lined up on top, holding the rubber roof slats in place when the wind blew. I counted those slats over and over. The tires represented the ridiculousness of the life I was living. I began to make up a rhyme as I continued to count them. "One, two, stupid you. Three, four, open the car door. Five, six, so tired of tricks. Seven, eight, is it too late? Nine, ten, will he do it again? STOP!" I told myself it was crazy to sit there and make up silly poems about my life. I was letting the utter absurdity of having to keep tires on the roof distract me. I shook my head to clear the emerging mantra out of my mind, took a big deep breath, and opened the car door with a loud creak.

I had decided to keep moving forward. I didn't know what the days ahead would hold, but I was going forward. I had suspected Ron's infidelity, but now I knew for certain. So many things that had not added up now did, and I hated the sum of all the lies over all the years. My husband had just confessed to cheating on me with both a stranger and a friend of mine. The moment no woman ever wants to live through was here; the nightmare had come to life.

Strangely, through the pain, I also felt a glimmer of hope that I had not felt in a long time. He finally told me the truth. He could have continued lying to me, but he didn't. Maybe he really was different. Something had changed inside of him; I could see that in our visits. He looked different - and he looked at me differently. There was a tenderness that had never been there before. Over the past 3 years, I had asked him that same question over and over again and always had received the same answer, "No." I knew he was lying all of those times; he could never look at me while emphatically saying "No." Now, here he was in prison, and finally he decided to tell me the truth. Surely he had to be wondering what effect his words would have on me, on our relationship.

Ron – Friendship is Sharing the Deepest Part of Yourself

I had to quiet the fear inside of me. Fear that this would cause her to leave me sitting here in a prison cell, alone. Fear that she would actively look for someone who could be all of the things to her that I could not be; a provider, a lover, a husband who kept his vows. I could not deny she deserved all of those things and so much more. But I couldn't help my own selfish feelings of wanting to hang onto her and our family. I desperately wanted the opportunity to make this up to her. I wanted to spend the rest of my life showing her that I did cherish her, that I was worthy of her love, faithfulness, and commitment. I wanted to be my wife's best friend.

Cathy – The Birth of Friendship Comes From the Death of Selfishness

Ron had to know what a risk he took in telling me everything that day. Although it may seem strange to say, Ron's confession saved our marriage. It was the death of our fragile, selfish, superficial marriage and the birth of a second chance for us. That conversation allowed us to strip away the entire pretense of our former existence and become emotionally, mentally and spiritually intimate as we journeyed through the next 15 years of Ron's imprisonment. Without the truth, we would never have been able to build a bridge between us in a way that gave us both strength and purpose. We would have fought each other instead of fighting FOR each other.

This whole experience made me realize how sometimes when friendship gets messy and difficult, it is the true test of the relationship's strength. It may not be an affair, but every couple will face a test of their friendship that will require them to define, or redefine, their own relationship. Real friendship takes effort. It makes us vulnerable. But when we give up our core selfishness, the result is a deeper transparency and a greater appreciation of the value of friendship.

In many ways, Ron's admission of guilt and my response to it was the tipping point for our marriage and family. And it continued to be at the edges of our relationship as several years later while out at a restaurant, I ran into the woman with whom Ron had been unfaithful. I saw the guarded look she gave me and the pain behind her bravado. I had forgiven Ron and I knew I needed to release her as well. I excused myself from my table and walked over to her. To her surprise, I asked if I could sit with her for a moment. As soon as I sat down, I held her hands in mine and told her that I knew what had happened; Ron had told me. "I forgive you. Ron says he is so sorry, and I am so sorry this happened. It has hurt me deeply, but I need you to know I forgive you." She immediately burst into tears and hung her head. She would not look at me; all false pride vanished and nothing but the pain of a wrong decision was left. I held her hands until she pulled them from my grasp. "Thank you," she whispered. Peace flooded through me. I quietly walked back to my table and away from the past. It was so freeing to forgive. I was so thankful that I knew Ron was not the same person he had been. I do not think I could have forgiven so easily had Ron still been the same selfish, broken man. But Ron had become a strong man, a man I deeply respected and loved. As he loved me and actively put forth the effort to rebuild our marriage, I was able to love, respect, and honor my husband.

Ron – Rebuilding Our Family While in Prison

As I reflect on the idea of friendship, especially the importance of shared moments, the strangest thoughts come to my mind. When it comes to shared experiences that build strong friendships, one of the greatest classrooms we found ourselves learning friendship in was in the prison visiting room. Wow! The stories and lessons that were created and learned in those moments set a new precedent for us. These times literally changed the course of our lives forever.

For up to 3 hours at a time it was just us. We were entirely focused on each other, and were a complete family unit; that was how we felt about a family visit in the prison. We came to a place of such appreciation and gratitude for each other that despite the lack of physical contact, our love for each other grew by leaps and bounds.

Right there, surrounded by other families visiting their loved ones, I came to a place in my relationship with Cathy that I could tell her anything and everything about me. In these visits, we learned to dream again. We learned to laugh with each other. We learned to be friends with each other. We learned to hurt for each other and cry for each other. We even learned to help each other when the world around us was falling apart and nobody seemed to notice.

One of the greatest challenges I was faced with was learning to help my wife work through her anger towards me. I had let her down. I was the reason why she was living as a single mother raising two boys on her own. She did not sign up for this. She and my two sons were innocent. I had to come to grips with the truth that I had robbed them of a life they deserved. Even though I was innocent of the crime of which I was convicted, the wrong choices I had made in my life led up to this moment. God's word tells us we will reap what we sow. Coming to understand the pain and suffering I had caused in my family's life also caused me to realize the sense of innocence that I had taken from my sons. They were now going to be exposed to a dark world that no child should ever step into. My job as a father was to protect my family from the dangers in the world, but because of my selfish behavior, I had exposed them to the world all alone, without the protection of their father.

The intensity of those moments of intimate friendship when I was with my family in the visiting room would keep me going for the next 10 days, until another visit was possible. The curious thing is that I lived more in those 3 hour visits than I did during the rest of the time in prison.

Ron – The Transformation of Our Lives
Through the Process of Friendship

Writing this chapter of the story of our lives has been by far the most difficult. I have searched for the words to tell you how I broke the heart of my bride, and I ask you, the reader, to forgive me for breaking my vow. I did not understand what the vow I had made truly meant. I did not know what true love and holy matrimony meant. How I wish I had not taken my vow lightly; how I regret my selfishness and ignorance. For all of those things, I am sorry.

Through our shared pain and suffering, through honest communication, our friendship was born. Cathy and I learned how to show true love for each other, even in the midst of the rubble of our circumstances. It was the birth of the success we now have in our marriage and in our lives, and this love stands strong and stable on the foundation of honesty and committed, loyal friendship.

Last summer Cathy and I were surprised by a most unusual opportunity. We got an engraved invitation to receive an award for our work. We were to be honored at the most unexpected place: The White House. This meant so much to us after all that we had been through. For Cathy, it also meant that she needed to purchase a suitable outfit! I went shopping with her, and she decided that she should try on all of the outfits she liked; so my job for the next twenty minutes was to stand by the ladies' dressing room and wait until she was done.

This isn't especially pleasant for me. This isn't even something that I can relate to. I'm a man. I own some great suits. Men's clothes don't go in and out of style. I always think I look great, so I don't worry about my clothes all that much. I don't feel the pressure that a woman does to set exactly the right tone with carefully chosen clothes. So, standing there, lost in a sea of dresses, I had to look for the potential good in sharing this interesting moment with Cathy. But, finding the right outfit for this kind of event was important to her, so that became enough of a reason for me to be there. When something is important to Cathy, she gets this certain look on her face, and in those moments all I want to do is let her know that I am there for her. I want her to know that I acknowledge the importance of this moment and I want to support her. Knowing this in my heart actually made standing outside the dressing room enjoyable.

In the experience of sharing, there are there are 3 things involved: "you," "me," and "us." Cathy loves to go to square dances. I do not like square dancing at all, but I love to be with my wife. So the "us" in this relationship goes square dancing. I plan the evenings and then have so much fun with my wife that no one knows I dislike it. It works the other way around, too. My wife hates sports, but she knows I like baseball. So what does the "us" do? We go watch a baseball game together. No one knows that Cathy doesn't like baseball except for me, because the "us" loves to be together and therefore we have a great time, a shared experience. Sharing is an opportunity you don't need to wait for. In order to build health into your family, just do it; share your experiences.

Cathy – The Commitment to "Us"

Maybe you have suffered a breach in your marriage. The breach could have been a sexual affair, an ongoing lack of respect, or a pattern of unfaithfulness of any kind. It is never too late to save a marriage if both of you are willing to put forth even a little effort. The trap so many marriages fall into is one of never letting the other partner move beyond the hurt or the event. When this happens, the marriage falls into a cycle of disrespect and unloving treatment of each other which compounds the injuries and extends the breach in the relationship.

Men need to feel respected and women need to feel loved. When a man feels disrespected, it is difficult for him to display love toward his partner. When a woman feels unloved, she typically lashes out in disrespect because she feels violated by the lack of love and attention. In an effort to protect herself, she actually deepens the divide by pushing her husband even further from her, making him feel even more disrespected and dishonored. A vicious cycle of disrespectful and unloving actions and words begins to further erode the foundation for a strong marriage.

In order to re-build a marriage after trauma (and even the seemingly small trauma of an argument must be repaired), the wife must purposefully treat her husband with respect and the husband must purposefully act lovingly towards his wife. Practice makes permanent; as we practice the foundational principles of a strong marriage, the marriage begins to get stronger. No longer do we have to make a conscious decision to act lovingly or respectfully; we have activated the friendship principle within our relationship that fosters the growth of our love and commitment toward each other. There is life after an affair and even after multiple affairs! And that life can become more rewarding and fulfilled if both are committed to each other and to the "us" of that relationship. Our family is stronger, healthier, and more vibrant than ever before. We have a deep appreciation of the love we share because we know what it is like to be in an uncaring marriage. Selfishness has no place in a strong marriage. Immature love and fragile foundations are built with selfish desires; lasting love and unshakeable family institutions are built with true commitment.

Ron and Bria – Sharing Rocks!

One of Bria's favorite things is to collect rocks. Whether on the beach or in a field, she enjoys finding uniquely colored and shaped stones. One day, I was looking for rocks with her. I really wanted to be engaged in pursuing her interests. So, I watched her pick up the rocks and exclaim what each rock looked like. "This one looks like a bird," she would say, "this one a canoe and this one looks like a heart."

I couldn't always see the resemblance, but I didn't want to admit that I could not see what she saw. Eventually, a unique-looking rock caught my attention. I picked it up and examined it. I was so excited. I said to her, "Look Bria! Look what I found! What would you call this?" She stopped her hunt and turned to look at my find.

"That's a rock, silly," she stated.

Sometimes things really are simply what they are. Friendship is the fiber that holds relationships together. Playing and laughing together allows us to build strength in the midst of everyday activities. That strength is what we draw from in order to recover from difficult times.

Practice Makes Permanent

Enjoy sharing with your spouse and family and watch your friendships thrive as you simultaneously build the resilience your family will need to overcome future adversity. Build your friendship through these easy activities:

- Affirm your spouse by saying 10 positive, true things to your partner every day.

- Tell your friends and family members at least 3 good things about your spouse every time you talk to them.

- Tell each of your children at least 10 positive things about themselves each day.

- Schedule one hour every day to spend with your family where you cannot be interrupted – no cell phones, no TV, just family doing fun "us" things that build friendship. (Build a fire, play a game, go on a walk, cook a meal together, etc.)

- Change the way your family functions together by changing your list of chores from things you HAVE to do to things you GET to do together. (We get to do the dishes, vacuum, dust, etc. together)

Doing these things will build harmony, love, and respect in your family. Before you know it, you will be amazed at the peace in your home and the fire in your relationship with your spouse!

Chapter 5
FAITHFULNESS

Faithfulness: affirming your family's intrinsic value, demonstrating steady allegiance to fulfilling your duty to protect, love and defend them.

Ron – Faithfulness Builds Trust, the Key to Friendship

In the modern world of "Housewives of Beverly Hills," it is easy to think that faithfulness is little more than abstaining from inappropriate sexual relationships. In reality, the level of trust necessary for people to share the deepest and most intimate aspects of themselves with other members of their family requires a much more complete understanding of faithfulness. Trust is the key to friendship, and faithfulness is the prerequisite of trust.

Cathy – Where has Faithfulness Gone?

When Ron was sentenced to 14-25 years in prison, I was stunned. I really had never considered that he might actually go to prison. I was alone with 2 small children and utterly terrified of what the future held for me and my family. The panic I felt as I considered living my life alone, having only brief, public contact with my husband in prison visiting rooms for the next 14-25 years, was superseded only by the intensity of my desire to protect and defend my children. As I looked down into their innocent faces and tried to explain to them that Daddy was in jail now, I felt the most intense need to rescue them from the sentence just pronounced over their lives. I was praying someone would show up and rescue me from this nightmare. Little did I know that God had a plan to rescue all of us out of the darkness in which we felt engulfed.

A few days after Ron was sentenced, someone knocked insistently on my door. I peeked out and recognized one of Ron's friends. As I opened the door, I was surprised to see him standing there alone on my front stoop. I did not consider him a friend of mine, but only of Ron's, but I warily

FRIENDSHIP
FAITHFULNESS
FORGIVENESS
FAIRNESS
FORTITUDE

opened the door to greet him. He began to ask how the boys and I were doing since Ron was in prison and asked to come in and talk with me for a while. I stood there looking intently at him. He must have misread the look on my face because his now featured a big cheesy smile as he explained that since Ron was in prison and he was here, he could help me in any way I needed. I felt a chill run through me as he stood there leering. This man actually thought I was going to welcome him into my home!

I felt betrayed by this man at my door, even though he was only an acquaintance. He was supposed to be a friend to my husband and here he was on my front step, obviously thinking he could establish a relationship with me while my husband was in prison. My stomach turned at the audacity of him coming to our home to prey on my grief and exploit Ron's absence. I didn't know whether to slap that look off of his face or to slam the door. I decided both were beneath me. I looked him in the eye and firmly explained that my policy was to never let a man in my home alone. He stood there with an incredulous look on his face and then reminded me that Ron would be gone for a very long time. "Exactly," I stated. "You may come back when he is home." He averted his eyes and then turned to walk away as I quietly but firmly closed the door. The most troubling part of that encounter was the fact that he had obviously never considered the fact that I would not let him in. How could he have thought that I would so easily allow another man to step into my home and my life? What I found even more despicable is that he was completely betraying his friendship to Ron. Was there to be no end of dishonor toward my husband, myself, and my family? Where was faithfulness? By closing the door on his invitation and publicly establishing my convictions and ground rules, I saved myself more battles. The precedent had been set and word got out.

Ron – Faithfulness Behind Bars

I was sitting in a prison cell, no longer able to play an active role in the lives of my wife and children. I was overcome with anger and grief that I would be a bystander, a mere spectator as lives unfolded before me.

Unable to protect my wife and children, I felt completely helpless and desperate to find a way to convey to Cathy how much I loved her and my sons. I fought the desperation in my heart. I longed to hold my family. I wanted nothing more than to hear my wife promise me that she would be faithful to me in all ways until I was released. I believed she loved me, but I could see the pain and grief in her eyes. Each time she came to visit me I could feel the depth of her loneliness and see the evidence of her exhaustion in the dark circles under her eyes. I felt disgusted with myself for thinking only of what I wanted and what I needed from her. This lifestyle was surely draining all of her energy, yet she stayed faithful. I didn't want to live in this dark place for decades knowing that she was unfulfilled and alone. I was enveloped in the regret that I had not shown Cathy how much she meant to me when I had so many opportunities to do so before I was locked up. I had completely taken her and my children for granted. I now wanted to be faithful to her and my sons. But, I realized I really did not even know what that word meant. I had never seen faithfulness in my home when I was growing up and I had no idea what commitment involved. I began talking to myself (in prison, you are allowed to do that) and asking myself, "What IS faithfulness?" I knew the answer in my heart. My wife is the very definition of faithfulness. She knows the meaning of that word deep in every fiber of her being. I also knew I did not have to ask her what faithfulness meant, I just had to watch how she lived every day. As I reflected on this I realized that faithfulness is not a single event for Cathy, or a perfume that she wears; it is part of the fragrance of her life. In the same way I had once been blind to her physical beauty, I realized that, even in marriage, I had consistently looked past her faithfulness to me and our family. Right before my eyes was a living manifestation of the thing I now so desperately wanted to understand.

From that moment forward, I determined that I would pour into my family every dream and inspiration I could find. I would be the lifter of their spirits and an encourager - a steady presence for them in the midst of the turbulence of their daily lives. I would be faithful to carry her, in every way I could, when she was too tired to walk. I determined to give everything to her and ask nothing from her.

Cathy – Making the Decision to be Faithful

Unsolicited advice was a constant and emotionally exhausting intrusion into my life as I considered what I should do to protect my children from as much harm as possible. Every visit we had together, I could see the question in Ron's eyes asking, "Will you wait for me?" Ron would lean across the small table between us, take my hands in his, squint his eyes slightly and look hard into my eyes. I knew he was looking for the strength to keep moving forward. I also knew I had precious little strength to spare as I managed his legal case, cared for our two small sons, and tried to deal with the seemingly insurmountable pile of bills. As the weeks moved slowly by, I had to take a long, hard look at my marriage and ask myself if I was prepared to honor my vows and wait for this man. Not just wait a year or two, mind you, but potentially for 25 years. The reality of carrying all the weight of this responsibility by myself and living apart for up to 25 years waged war against my desire to hold my family together. The battle wasn't about whether I loved my husband or believed in him; it was about me. The unspoken question constantly going through my mind was, "Who is going to take care of me?"

As I wrestled with the question of who would care for me if I chose to remain faithful to my husband, I realized that I had already made the decision to spend my life married to Ron when I said "I do." I wanted to pretend that I was making a new decision, because this situation could not possibly fit under the original "I do." I had not understood the depth of the meaning of those two words until just then. "I do." It had a period at the end of it and was not followed by an "unless . . . ." Ron was doing all he could to pour his heart and soul into my life and our children's lives in spite of the distance. He seldom complained about his own situation and rarely talked about how his life was inside the prison walls. He did, however, look to me for strength; the strength that comes from knowing someone is faithful and true. Strength to make it through this terrible ordeal and strength that comes from having someone walk through the storm with you. I knew he loved me and our children and that he longed to care for us and protect us. I also knew we could make our marriage work and hold our family together in spite of the obstacles if we would commit to the effort to make it happen. I finally admitted that there could be no question about my faithfulness. The answer had already been given in 1986 when we were married. I would remain faithful to Ron and fight for our family to grow stronger in spite of the distance, even if that meant I would have to live apart from my husband for the next quarter of a century.

Ron and Bria - That Spot is Reserved!

As you might expect from all we learned through our ordeals, we speak frequently about what faithfulness is and how important it is to be faithful in life. One evening, when Bria was just seven years old, I ran up the steps to tuck her into bed. I had traveled that day and so I did not arrive home until late. She was already in bed; but I knew that she wouldn't be asleep. I entered her room to give her a kiss and pray with her before she fell asleep. I walked over to sit on the edge of her bed as I asked if she would like to pray with me. But as soon as I sat down, she sat straight up and demanded, "Get off my bed! You cannot sit on my bed. I am saving that spot for my husband."

Although it was rather surprising, I was struck by this beautiful confirmation that she was already learning the importance of faithfulness as she was preparing a place in her life that was reserved only for her future husband.

Exercising Faithfulness

Faithfulness is not an optional part of marriage. It is not something that can be turned off and on. Conditional faithfulness is simply unfaithfulness by another name. I know a man who exercises for about one week every year - the week before he goes to see his doctor for an annual checkup. His doctor tells him at every checkup that he needs more exercise. Even though he has lived an unhealthy lifestyle for most of his life, this man could choose to build his health by exercising regularly rather than just hitting the gym before appointments. Offering conditional faithfulness is like someone who takes care of his body only when he needs something from it, or when he needs it to perform; otherwise he feels free to abuse it. Conditional faithfulness is not really faithfulness at all; it proceeds from selfishness, and it cannot produce a healthy family. Genuine faithfulness is the cornerstone of a solid marriage and family.

FRIENDSHIP
FAITHFULNESS
FORGIVENESS
FAIRNESS
FORTITUDE

Ron – Faithfulness is Security

As the hours I spent behind bars turned into days and the days turned into years, I watched how the men around me managed to survive in this place. It didn't take me long to figure out that the rules were different here; men were being beaten nearly to death for a debt of only a dime. I was determined to keep to myself and not get caught up in any of the daily arguments that always led to violence. One day, there was an altercation between two Muslims and a Latino in the weight room. I don't know how the fight started, but the word was that as the Latino came into the weight room, the two Muslims attacked him and began to beat him. As the fight continued, one of the Muslims held him down while the other man slammed the weights down on his hand; he lost his fingers after the weight of the plates crushed his hand. Everyone knew this would lead to serious retaliation from the Latinos. The altercation had added to the already strained racial tension throughout the prison. The whispers in the dark were of allegiance to one side or the other as plans were made for revenge against those who had orchestrated the attack.

As the tension grew, all the Latinos were asked if we wanted to be transferred to another prison or stay. I chose to stay. As I tried to simply go about my own business each day, it became more and more clear that battle lines were being drawn, and that the powder keg would soon ignite. I was in the cafeteria line getting my food when I heard someone call my name. I turned to look and saw the leader of the Latino group. "Come here, Tijerina, I want to talk to you," he said in Spanish. As I turned toward his voice, I was surprised to see a group of men waiting for me. I knew that he was confronting me to find out which side I would take when the fight broke out. I walked confidently over to him in spite of the nervousness building up inside of me. "What's up?" I asked. "You know what is about to go down and I need to know whose side you are going to be on when it happens." came the reply.

He looked me straight in the eyes, trying to gauge if I was going to be with him or against him. I paused to say a quick prayer and think about how to answer this challenge. I heard God's voice in my spirit telling me to turn my response back on him. I said, "Tell me which side Jesus is going to be on; that is the side I will be on." He looked at me dumbfounded. "What?" he asked incredulously. "Ah, TJ, man, you always talk like this." he declared as he walked away. Never again was my loyalty questioned. Everyone knew where I would stand when lines were drawn. More importantly, I knew where I stood. My lifestyle told everyone else that I was firm in my convictions to follow Christ. I knew the source of faithfulness was Christ. I had invited Him into my heart and my life the day I was convicted and I had spent my time in prison learning about Him and sharing my faith.

Living by my convictions made it possible to defend my ground when I was challenged. This is faithfulness. When you live your life exemplifying faithfulness, the challenges are fewer and the battles are more likely to be won. Faithfulness means to protect and defend, every time. There was a time I believed people did not have a choice about faithfulness; they either were or they weren't. I thought it was an innate personality trait; you either had a predisposition toward faithfulness or you didn't. I was wrong. Faithfulness is a choice. It is a decision you make when you enter into any relationship that is of value to you. It is never too late to embrace faithfulness. It creates in you a reputation that precedes you and defines you. It brings trust. It provides safety.

Cathy – Living out True Faithfulness

It was not difficult to be faithful to Ron by my own definition of the word. I never had an affair of any kind—I was very careful to avoid any appearance of inappropriate behavior in my relationships. So I thought

I had faithfulness mastered. If only it were that simple! Faithfulness is so much more than what most people assume it is. Though for most people, this concept would involve sexual misconduct or an affair, either emotional or physical, that definition stops so far short of the true meaning of faithfulness! I believe it means living out the belief in your family's intrinsic value, demonstrating a steady allegiance and thoroughly performing your duty to protect, love, and defend the members of your family. When I had to look at myself in light of this definition, I was struck with the realization that I had not been as faithful as I had thought.

Soon after Ron went to prison, I began looking for another home to rent. I desperately wanted to move out of the trailer that we had lived in together out in the country. As I hunted for homes, I found one I really liked. I called the owner and set up an appointment to see the house. It was everything I wanted. It was a big, neat, clean home with a sunny kitchen and a large yard for the boys to play in. I loved it! As we finished the tour and I told the owner I was very interested, he began to pre-qualify me as a potential renter. "Are you married?" he asked. I told him I was very happily married as matter of fact. "What does your husband do for a living?" was the next question. Oh my! How should I answer that question? I didn't want him disqualifying me simply because Ron was in prison, and I would certainly have to explain the whole entire scenario of Ron's conviction if I mentioned it. I really did not want to spend the next 45 minutes discussing Ron's case. "Um, my husband is serving." I answered as evasively as I could. "Serving? Like in the military?" he persisted with his questions. "Um, yes, kind of…He is in the ministry while he is serving," I stammered. I consoled myself that it really was only a half-lie since I considered that my husband indeed was ministering to others while in prison serving his time. The home owner was excited about that answer and didn't ask any more questions. As I walked back to my car holding hands with my two small sons, I had to admit I had just lied. And worse than that, I had been unfaithful to my husband. I had been embarrassed by the circumstances of our lives and, by disguising the truth, had not demonstrated a steady allegiance to him or my family.

I tried so hard to justify the lie and to reason away the nagging feeling of guilt in my heart. Later that evening, I received a phone call from one of my friends whom I had listed as a reference. She was so hurt and disappointed in me for telling a lie about my family, and she was angry that I had embarrassed her by giving her name as a reference after lying. Not only had I been unfaithful to my husband and family, that unfaithfulness had rippled out to affect my friend. I determined to never let that happen again. I never wanted to let fear of what other people think keep me from living out my steady allegiance to my husband and family again – not the fear of what a potential landlord would think, what opportunities I might lose, or what anyone else's opinion would be of my family. I pledged that my husband's name would be safe in my mouth – in my every word. I would honor him in my speech; being careful of how I spoke of him, I was ready to live out the kind of faithfulness that creates safety and stability.

Brandon – Faithfulness Creates Security

Faithfulness is a word that seems to have lost its meaning and importance, not only in relationships, but also in families. I was in the store the other day and saw on the cover of a magazine an intriguing announcement: Celebrity moms were being voted on as either good or bad. By whose standard, I wondered? It made me think about my own parents and childhood. When I was a child my family literally had no money. I had no idea, however, that we were the "poor family." My dad was in prison, and my mom was on welfare, yet my brother and I wouldn't have wanted to be in any other family. I loved my parents and that my mom loved spending time with me. My mom showed my brother and I what faithfulness really looked like. She was loyal and steadfast in the hard journey that was our life. She fought hard to keep her family intact. She always believed that through a miracle, my dad would be released from prison and we would all be together again. (I don't think she ever thought it would really take a full fifteen years.) As the years slowly unfolded, and prison visits continued, my mother's confidence impacted me less, and I began to lose hope that my dad would ever be released from behind those iron gates.

As hope that my dad would be part of my childhood faded, I began to have this recurring dream. In this dream, I had visions of Christmas. The house was filled with decorations of the nativity scene, snowmen, and Santa. The tree was all lit up with a large assortment of different colored lights, the sweet smell of cinnamon rolls filled the air, and there were two big piles of presents. One pile was for me and the other pile was for my brother. As it is in dreams, everything was exactly how a picture perfect Christmas should be.

As it continued, my brother and I took turns opening presents so that our mom could take a picture of us with a new toy, clothes, or a game. My brother was the first to open a present since he is older. Finally, it was my turn. I opened my first present, and it was a Superman toy. I loved, and still do, love Superman. He has all this power to do whatever he wants, but instead of being one of the villains, he chooses to be a hero. I could talk about the fantastic attributes of Superman all day! After I had a picture taken with my new toy, I opened it and went to my room to play with all of my other action figures and Superman, naturally, the most important superhero of them all.

As I was playing with my toys, I realized that I had forgotten to open my other presents. So I went back to the living room for the rest of my gifts, but I was stopped short. In this dream, I heard my mom laughing in the kitchen. I quickly jumped behind the tree to hide because I heard an unfamiliar voice with hers. I then saw my mom walking into the living room with a man that wasn't my dad. My heart sank, and I froze. I just sat there waiting for the perfect time to get out and run away. After deciding there wasn't going to be a good time for me to reveal myself, I just jumped out and started yelling at my mom and this unknown guy and then ran outside. My mom didn't even run after me right away. She had the audacity to apologize to this guy for the way I reacted towards him and then came after me, acting like everything was just fine.

"My mom showed my brother and I what faithfulness really looked like."

66

I stood in the yard yelling at her. "I'm running away! I can't believe you would do that to us!" So I started running, but I couldn't run fast. It felt like something was holding me back and not allowing me to run as fast as I knew I could. I was concentrating so hard to make my body move faster, but the harder I tried the slower I went. Eventually my mom would catch up to me, and then I would wake up.

I had this dream turned nightmare several times while growing up. Having your parents split up is a child's worst nightmare, and I kept thinking that that dream was too real for it to not mean anything. Every time that thought would enter my mind, it felt like my stomach was in my throat. I kept that dream to myself and tried not to think of it, but I was unsuccessful. I believed in my heart that it was only a matter of time until it turned into a reality. I thank God that it never did!

Children need to know that parents are who they claim to be. My mom, by the way she lived her life, calmed my unreasonable, but understandable fears, and eventually those awful nightmares stopped. My mom's continued, day after day, faithfulness to our family is what helped my brother and me get through the hell that was our lives.

> "Children need to know that parents are who they claim to be."

I am convinced that anyone can become faithful. As my dad tells me all the time, "Your past does not define you, but it can qualify you for your future if you let it." Regardless of what your past has been, your future can be different.

Faithfulness is a Choice

Everyone is faced with opportunities to demonstrate faithfulness each day. Do we lovingly do all we can to protect, defend, and love each other or do we expose, hurt, and betray one another? Faithfulness is a decision; it is a choice we make. It is the first step in building a strong family. The ability to stand resolute with one another in spite of faults, flaws, and adversity brings strength and trust into the equation of strong families. It is the cornerstone of a family. The value of faithfulness cannot be minimized. Without it, we are just a group of related, but self-centered, inconsistent people fighting and limping our way down the road of life, ultimately alone.

Faithfulness of the Heart

When we work with other families who want to rebuild or rejuvenate their lives and marriages, we always stress that your family members must know that their name is safe in your mouth. Can your spouse and children say that of you? Are they safe, or do you tear them down or criticize them with your words and the way you talk about them when they aren't around?

What is in our hearts will come out of our mouths, so the heart is the first place to build faithfulness. Faithfulness of the heart is a choice, and that choice is then reflected in how we think about and then talk about one another. Over the years it has been amazing to see the tremendous changes that occur in the families that we work with when couples choose to be faithful to one another through their thoughts and words.

Cathy and Bria – Papa's Most Important Job

Bria was four years old and skipping up the steps slowly because her legs where too short to move very quickly. She turned to me and said, "Momma, do you know what Papa's job is?"

I looked down at her big, round, shining eyes and replied, "I think I do, but I am not sure. What is Papa's job, Bria?"
She stopped her ascent and turned to look me in the eye. She announced with great authority, "Papa's job is to catch us if we start to fall."

"Yes, yes it is!" I replied as I thought how very right she was.

Practice Makes Permanent

We each depend upon the other to catch us if we start to fall. When you make mistakes, and you will, it is faithfulness that comes to your rescue.

Are your loved one's names safe in your mouth?

Do you consistently bless them with your words and choose your words carefully when you say their names whether they are present or not?

Faithfulness sees the imperfections, but chooses to ignore them and focus on how to protect, love and defend the imperfect members of a permanent family.

When you have worked hard to make your family healthy, safety and peace are established by faithfulness.

Demonstrate faithfulness in your relationships by using these techniques:

Ask yourself these three questions when you are tempted to be unfaithful in your words or actions. If any of your answers are, "No," choose a more faithful course of action. If the answer is that it is neutral or honorable, it is safe to proceed. This simple step will take less than one minute and will save you and your family from the poison of unfaithfulness. We have heard from thousands of couples whose relationships were transformed simply by following this one piece of advice.

Will this bring honor to my family?

Will this bring honor to my spouse?

Will this bring honor to me?

FRIENDSHIP

FAITHFULNESS

FORGIVENESS

FAIRNESS

FORTITUDE

Take time today to make a list of things you need to change in order to demonstrate a steady allegiance to protect, love, and defend your family. Perhaps it is refraining from pointing out your spouse's faults to others, or maybe it is remaining silent or saying something encouraging instead of criticizing when your loved one makes a mistake. Whether it is a seemingly small unfaithfulness or a big, glaring unfaithfulness, it is poisoning your family and weakening your relationships. By taking the time to purposefully invest in being faithful in all ways, you will rebuild your family's foundation and create an environment which will enable your family to thrive.

Commit to apologize to your loved ones for being unfaithful to them. Every person has exhibited unfaithfulness toward their loved ones at some time in their relationship. Whether it is a single event or an ongoing pattern of behavior, you owe your loved one honesty and an apology for your unfaithfulness. Take the time to explain to them why your actions or words were unfaithful. Let them know of your commitment to protect them and your relationship in the future. Example: Set up a family meeting.

Activate faithfulness in your family by setting aside time to stay connected. Set aside 4 hours a week to purposefully connect to each other – 2 hours talking and building bridges and 2 hours playing together (collaborate with your family to plan your play).

Forgiveness – The ability to move beyond the offenses from others and experience the freedom that comes from releasing others for the larger purpose of family strength.

Ron – The Healing Power of Forgiveness

Forgiveness is to the health of a family the same as physical healing is to the body. We all need healing because injury is unavoidable. As necessary as it is for sharing and friendship within family relationships, we all sometimes fail to be faithful in one manner or another. So when offenses come, it is important that healing take place. And because we are human and fail often, the healing balm of forgiveness has to be a part of our daily experience. If it is not, bitterness is the result. Bitterness has the destructive power to poison other people like an infection. And it follows that members of a family who refuse to practice forgiveness will inevitably have unfulfilled lives, and contribute to the disintegration of their families.

There is an old expression that, "Time heals all wounds." It isn't true; only good choices and right attitudes are capable of healing all wounds. Without the positive choice of forgiveness, the only things that grow over time are scars and bitterness. It's important to understand that healing does take time, but the pain and isolation that come when family members injure one another never just goes away automatically. Failure isolates one person from another and requires reconciliation, not just the passage of time. If you want health in your family, then, it is imperative that everyone work towards forgiveness and reconciliation.

Today, true forgiveness in families seems to be disappearing. Our society has made it much simpler to dispose of relationships that are uncomfortable. Cathy and I contend that there is no such thing as a disposable person or disposable family relationship! The test for whether or not you are living in forgiveness is this: have you done everything in YOUR

FRIENDSHIP

FAITHFULNESS

FORGIVENESS

FAIRNESS

FORTITUDE

power to live at peace with everyone? Very few people look for the ways they have contributed to a problem in a relationship and ask forgiveness for their part. When you do this and reach out to the other person, it makes it much easier for the other person to ask forgiveness for their part. The most freeing part of the process is that even if the other person will not ask forgiveness or seek reconciliation, you are free from guilt and have a clear conscience, knowing that you did the right thing! There is nothing like the relief of guilt being taken away.

Living in forgiveness is not dependent upon the offender accepting the forgiveness, adjusting their behaviors, and choosing to do all they can to be a better person. It is only dependent upon our ability to do everything within our power to live at peace. It is critical to understand that when I have been offended by another member of my family, I cannot change the other person. Forgiveness isn't accomplished by showing the offender the nature and extent of their failure. It is accomplished by letting the person know that even though I feel injured and I need time to recover from my injury, I desire healing in the relationship; I don't want to be separated forever. I would be lying if I said that this is an easy thing to do. While it may be simple to understand, it is very difficult to actually do. However, without forgiveness, most families fall prey to the destruction that comes from bitterness.

As you read our stories, think about the situations in your own life where you have had to make a tough decision to offer forgiveness or, perhaps, those times you have been consumed by bitterness. Consider what effect these decisions have had on your relationships. Our experience has taught us that the journey to forgiveness is a long one, but it can be filled with freedom, and with wondrous opportunities for growing a really deep level of family connectedness.

Ron – The Verdict

"Guilty."

Speechless, dizzy, and numb—but most of all shock are the words that only barely describe how I was feeling when the judge read the verdict: GUILTY. I did not understand what was happening; I could not comprehend the meaning of what was said. It all happened so fast! Yet, ironically, everything around me seemed to be moving in slow motion. When the judge finished reading the verdict, he ordered the deputy to take me into custody. As I turned slowly to face my family and friends, the deputy approached me. He told me to extend my arms out and then he handcuffed me. Part of me wanted to lie on the floor and curl up in a ball to become invisible. Fear began its tight grip on me.

My eyes were open, yet everything in front of me became a blur. It was as if all went blinding white around me. I could barely stand. I then felt two very soft, gentle hands on my face. As my sight returned I saw it was my wife, Cathy. She was doing her best to reassure me. She kept saying, "It is going to be okay. We are going to get you out." I could hear in her voice both anger and determination, but it was fear I saw in her eyes. She put her arms around me, holding me tight as she told me she loved me. I was going to prison because of an unjust and unfounded accusation from my wife's unstable, teenaged relative. All I could say back to her over and over again was, "But he lied." I then saw myself being pulled far away from the world I lived in, seeing a vortex all around me. I heard Cathy say, "I know he lied. It is going to be okay. We are going to get you out. I promise. Hang on, Ron."

Off in the distance I heard a man weeping like a child. He was wailing in pain. I turned blankly to see who was crying for me; it was a dear friend, who had been like a second father to me. He had a greater understanding of what was happening than I did in that moment and wept for me, my wife, my children and our shattered lives. I believe that at some point, everyone asks themselves, "Who will cry at my funeral?" Hearing my family and friends weep, I thought about death. My life as I had known it was slain, and this was the funeral. My dear friend walked up to me and held me as if I were his very own little boy that was being taken from him. My heart and mind steadied, and I was filled with gratitude for this man who was weeping for me when I could not yet cry.

I turned to kiss my wife and mother good-bye. As I kissed Cathy good-bye, everything seemed to be moving away from me. I still could not wrap my mind around what was really happening. I told Cathy, "Tell the boys I love them. I love you, Cathy." As I turned to leave, I was wondering, "Who is going to take care of my family?" I thought, "I need to see my sons. I need to hold them, to tell them I love them and that everything will be OK. Somebody help me! Somebody help my family!"

I was taken out of the court room, cuffed and directed into the front seat of an unmarked police car. "But I didn't do it. He lied." I repeated those words over and over, but they fell on deaf ears. This could not possibly be happening to me. My mind was reeling from the impact of hearing the word "guilty" come out of the judge's mouth. This must be a nightmare. This does not happen in real life. People do not go to prison for things they did not do. Only guilty people go to prison! I was riding in a police car trying to catch my breath. Then I was sitting in a hard plastic chair wondering what waited for me on the other side of the door. The next thing I knew, someone was instructing me to undress in front of a guard. I was still in shock that I was going to prison. I began to remove my clothes and anger began its journey into my heart.

With each movement, anger crept deeper into my body. I wasn't even fighting against the bitterness that moved in that day. I had just been robbed of my freedom, my family and my reputation. I was so completely terrified and in shock that I had just been found guilty of something I had not done. If anyone had a right to be angry and withhold forgiveness, it was me! I had just watched members of my wife's family, because of their own resentment and prejudice, take the stand and lie about me. They would not look at me, but looked at the jury and convinced them with their stories that I was the villain and was guilty of heinous crimes. Seeing the looks of horror and disgust on the faces of those in the jury box told me they believed the lies they were hearing. I wanted to interrupt and tell them all about how this made-up story had begun and continued to grow until it was the monstrous lie they were hearing at this trial. I had wanted to put a stop to the outrageousness of it all; but I had to remain silent as the tale was woven and the stories that would rob me of my freedom were told.

My attorney had recommended that we should not call our witnesses; he believed the stories were so obviously lies that I would not be convicted. Now I was here, sitting in a prison cell, not fully understanding the impact of the verdict on my own life, let alone the impact it would have on my wife and on our children. I knew only that I had been taken away from them. My conviction would impact my family and me for the rest of our lives. But even then, I still was seeing only the tip of the iceberg.

Cathy – How Can They Do This?

I listened to the verdict being read and was struck to my core with shock. I watched in horror as the color drained from Ron's face. I watched him begin to sway and lose his balance as the judge continued to read the word "guilty" over and over. I couldn't even go to him, stand next to him, or hold his hand; I could do nothing but stand in horror and watch the events play out in front of me. Our attorney reached over to steady Ron so he could remain standing for the rest of the reading of the verdict. "Stop!!" my mind was screaming, but the words thankfully did not escape my lips. The members of my own family had done this to us. How could one have fabricated – and another believed – such a lie?

The nightmare continued to unfold as the judge ordered the Deputy to take Ron into custody. I watched as he took each of Ron's hands and clicked the metal handcuffs around his wrists. I rushed over to my husband as soon as I was granted permission to approach him. The shock that was reeling through everyone in the courtroom had overtaken Ron. He looked through me with disbelief at his new fate, telling me over and over again, "But he lied." I just wanted to go home with my husband. I wanted to walk out of those doors holding hands, walk out to our car and drive away from this madness. Instead, I held his face in my hands and tried to reassure him that we would fix this terrible mistake. Before I could say all I wanted to, though, we were kissing good-bye and they were escorting Ron off to prison. I walked out of the courtroom with

the dozens of other people who sat through the trial. I heard Ron's mother weeping, a dear friend wailing, and others talking in angry, low voices, but I was numb. I had just watched my husband be convicted of a crime I absolutely knew he did not commit and then be cuffed and taken off to prison.

I stepped into the hallway, disoriented. I looked at the people slowly moving down the hallway away from the courtroom. "Back to their normal lives," I thought to myself as I stood in the rubble of what had been my life. I turned and saw a window at the end of the hall and it dawned on me that as I stood there, Ron was being led away. I rushed over to the window, and with my face pressed against the cool glass, I watched the police car drive away with my husband inside. The first of many tears escaped my eyelashes and trailed down my cheek. As the car disappeared, I slowly turned back and stared down the now empty hall. I was alone. My thoughts turned to our children. My sons! What about my sons? How would they bear the separation from their father? How was I going to explain this to them? Anger began to well up inside of me. My own relative had started this lie and then another one had not only carried it, but also added to it. How dare they do this to us? I was convinced I would not, could not, ever forgive them for what they had done to my family. The pain was unbearable. I stood rooted to the spot by the window, watching the car disappear with my husband in it. I wasn't even aware that bitterness was beginning to penetrate my heart and life.

Ron – The Beginning of Life Outside the Box

Thankfully, it didn't take me long to realize being angry and bitter was going to destroy me. I had to believe that this was happening to us for a reason so much bigger than my family and I could see right then. As the guard escorted me to my cell on the first floor, the door buzzed open and he waved me in. The corrections officer closed the door behind me, and I felt it lock inside of me; click is what I heard; SLAM is what I felt. I stood there with shock and fear ripping me apart. I know it was only the hand of God that kept me together. I began to look around. As I walked in, to my left was a stainless steel toilet and next to it was a stainless steel sink. The wall was recessed slightly so that the bed was not in the middle of the floor. The bed was a steel frame holding a simple mattress. In front of the bed was a desk with slots to put clothes or other belongings in, and there was a dimmer knob for the light, but not an on/off switch. After standing there for about 5 minutes trying to get my bearings, I walked into the cell and dropped my assigned sheets and clothes onto the bed. I then dropped to my knees, and for the first time since this began, I started to cry, calling out to God to help me. I didn't know what was going to happen next, but I somehow knew in my heart that God was the only one who could take care of me and my family. In that moment, I committed my life to Jesus.

I began to pray for my family and for Aaron, who had lied. At first my motive in praying for him was purely selfish – so I could get out and go home to my family. I wanted Aaron, who had so wronged me, to confess that he lied to everyone. As time went on, however, my Christian faith began to really deepen, and I began to pattern my life after Jesus. In doing so I began to forgive all those who had a part in putting me in prison, including my wife's relatives. As I started to realize that God had a purpose for allowing this to happen to me and my family, I knew I had to completely surrender to that purpose or I would be swallowed up by bitterness. I slowly saw the truth of what was happening. Here I was in a physical prison and my primary accuser was out in the free world, but I was truly freer than he was. He was trapped in a prison built by a lie that he could not get out of and was drowning in the guilt and pain of it.

Coming to a place in my heart of totally forgiving was not a simple process. A fierce battle raged inside me for quite some time. Days would go by that I never thought about the man who lied, but then I would sit on my bed and look at pictures and see my sons growing up without me. I would see them learning how to ride bikes, learning how to throw a baseball, and teaching themselves how to shave. I would hear about them asking each other about girls.

I couldn't even be a spectator in their lives! I was put away from them and missing every milestone in their lives. In moments like this, I would begin getting angry at Aaron all over again. But as the days moved slowly by, I realized I couldn't waste my energy on feeding the hate and the poison of bitterness that preyed on the only strength I had. I knew it would take a lot of energy to try to keep my family together from within the walls. I prayed, "Lord, please take care of my family and please help me become the husband and father I should have been." Strangely, I felt compassion for the untruthful young man whose despicable words had put me in prison. I knew his prison was actually far worse than mine. I began to pray even more for him, and forgiveness became stronger and stronger until it reigned in my heart with peace. When we are willing to consider someone else's feelings and experiences in the midst of our own pain, it becomes much easier to forgive and the pain is much easier to bear.

Cathy – *The Journey to Forgiveness*

My first stop on my way home from the trial was to confront Aaron about the lies he had just told. Even though we had been close, I looked him in the eye and told him that I would never, ever forgive him for what he had just done. As I left him, I felt a deep sadness grip my heart. I had loved him and would have done anything for him. In fact, I had provided a home for him when it was needed; I had invested in his life.

I wept for the loss of my relationship as I left this misguided teenager that day. I knew bitterness would come with a high price, but I convinced myself that I was willing to pay it and therefore did not have to forgive him, his mother, the misguided judge, the overzealous prosecutor, or anyone involved in this miscarriage of justice. I soon learned I was so very wrong. Bitterness has a way of eating away at your soul. It slinks around and devours every piece of joy or happiness and leaves the stench of a wasted life behind it; a life wasted on destructive feelings, time wasted on recounting wrongs and adding up offenses; time that could have been spent building a foundation of joy and happiness.

For me, the first casualty of that bitterness was laughter. It is impossible to laugh when anger and bitterness crowd out any joy or happiness. I soon discovered what a sad life it is to find fault in everything and to be discontent all the time because of the tragedy I believed I was stuck in. Yet I stubbornly tried to hold onto my right to be bitter and hold a grudge. I looked at what I had lost and how I had suffered and felt entitled to feel angry – and not just for myself, but for my children! Eventually, though, it became apparent that I could not rebuild our family while dragging this bitterness around with me. It would seep into every moment and steal away a happy memory or the magic of a special occasion. All my attention and energy was spent on fueling the fire of my resentment and pain. It was exhausting, but I couldn't imagine how to live without this anger filling my heart.

One day, after we returned from a long drive to visit Ron in prison, Brandon ran into the house, grabbed a blanket, and then climbed up into what had been Ron's chair. He carefully tucked the blanket around his little body, pressed his face against the chair and started talking to the chair. I asked him what he was doing. He informed me that he was pretending that Daddy was holding him and they were talking about all the fun things they were going to do when Daddy came home. Then he said, "And we are not talking about being mad that Daddy was gone. We don't have time to be sad because we are too busy being happy together."

He was smiling up at me looking so very content in the midst of his imaginary encounter with his father. I was struck by the simplicity of what he had just said. We don't have time to be sad because we are too busy being happy. I longed to be happy and not carry the hurt and pain. It was such hard work to carry anger and bitterness around all the time, but it was also hard to let go. I wanted my sons to grow up holding onto the ideal that it is easier to forgive and be happy than to hold onto an offense and be miserable, but it was a challenge to live that out. I had to make a decision to forgive, and I was struggling against myself to make that decision. I was wronged and my family was suffering as a result of that wrong. However, I realized that my family was suffering even more because I was adding anger and bitterness to the injustice we were already living through. I was making it impossible to be happy

FRIENDSHIP

FAITHFULNESS

FORGIVENESS

FAIRNESS

FORTITUDE

because I was so busy being angry! It dawned on me that our journey would be so much easier to navigate if we could make as many happy memories as possible along the way and enjoy life as much as possible instead of always focusing on our loss. I didn't want to poison my children with hate and bitterness; I wanted them to grow up to be compassionate and loving men and fathers.

So, I began practicing forgiveness. Every time I wanted to talk about all that had been taken from us, I talked about all the good things we had together instead. When I was frustrated or disappointed, I gave myself one week to get over it and then I disciplined myself to move on so that we could focus on the more important things in life. I began to look at people differently and to have compassion for those who hurt others because of their own pain. I saw my own relatives differently. I saw one as frightened and protective as she heard the lies told to her. She simply could not believe someone who married into the family over one who was born into it. And she found it impossible that her son could fabricate such a terrible tale. As I looked at the young men closest to me, my own two sons, I could understand her pain and her passion, and I allowed myself to forgive her and experience love for her again.

> *"I stopped thinking about how much I was losing and started discovering the beauty of my life."*

As I released the bitterness I had been carrying, I began to laugh again! It was the sweetest feeling to be able to throw my head back and hear laughter coming from myself. As I looked back on that time of focusing all my energy on feeding my bitterness, I realized that it had been less than a year, but it seemed like decades. I stopped fueling the pain and anger every time I saw someone who had been involved in Ron's imprisonment. I stopped thinking about how much I was losing and started discovering the beauty of my life. It was a constant battle, but we kept holding onto forgiveness in spite of all the times pain threatened to destroy our lives. I had a husband that loved me and inspired me to be a better person all the time, two amazing children and a brand new opportunity to build a good life for my children. Forgiveness was what

80

we needed in order to bond as a family and build joyful memories in the midst of the 15 years apart. As a family, we learned that forgiveness is a journey and we courageously chose to walk down that path together every day.

Cathy – Blake's Forgiveness Epiphany

In 2001, Blake, who was 14 at the time, missed Ron terribly. His dad had been in prison for ten years and was finally up to be reviewed by the parole board. Blake felt he needed his dad home more than anything else in his life. He would say, "I know my dad is innocent. If they would just listen to us, Dad could come home." Unfortunately, Martha, Aaron's mother, disagreed and actively fought to keep Ron in prison. Time after time, over an entire decade, Blake watched as motions were denied and appeals were lost on his father's case. Martha doggedly wrote letters and attended hearings in opposition to his father's release as she fought to keep his father's case from being overturned. As the hearing approached, Blake decided he had to confess his feelings of anger and hurt with this woman, whom he loved in spite of their differences about his father. He met with her and shared all of his feelings and then asked her to please stop fighting and let the courts decide his father's future and not attend the upcoming hearing. Much to his surprise and relief, she agreed. However, on the day of the hearing, Blake watched as she walked into the courtroom to oppose his father's release.

I saw the color drain out of Blake's face. He leaned forward, staring at Martha, daring her, maybe begging her, to look at him. She refused to meet his eyes. Later that evening, Blake stormed to his room declaring he completely disowned this much-loved relative and that he would never again speak to her nor see her as long as he lived. I wept for the pain of seeing my son so wounded and cried out to God to somehow heal the pain that I knew was in Blake's heart and spirit. I also struggled with the pain and disappointment in my own heart. Waves of anger washed over me as I considered the injustice of it all. My husband was sent to prison for a crime he did not commit. My innocent sons were constantly battling against discrimination as children of an inmate. Now this rejection and broken promise threatened to break the fragile thread of hope we were spinning for our futures. I curled up in my bed, hugging my pillow against me and wept quietly so my sons would not hear my anguish. Later that night, Blake woke me up, weeping. "Mom, Mom! I have to talk to you." With a soft, broken voice, my fourteen year old son explained, "I was telling God I was done; done hoping, done believing that anything good was ever going to happen to me. I am just so tired of being hurt, lied to, overlooked, and ignored. He let me throw a big temper tantrum before he asked me one question: 'Blake, do you want to be bread or butter?' I know it sounds crazy. But I know what I heard in my heart. I felt God tell me that I have two choices. I can choose to be like bread or I can choose to be like butter. He is letting me decide. I knew what He was saying to me. If I choose to be like bread, he showed me what would happen. When bread is left out, it gets hard and crumbles when the least bit of pressure is rubbed against it. If it gets wet, it disintegrates and disappears. It becomes useless and stale, leaving no trace behind. He showed me what will happen if I choose to be like butter. When butter is left out and melts, it can soften the hardest bread. It won't dissolve in water, and it leaves a mark on whatever it touches. He is asking me to be like butter for Martha's sake, to let Him use me and my life to soften her heart toward Him and to impact others whose lives I touch for His glory."

He stopped for a moment to catch his breath as the sobs broke free from his throat. "It is so hard, but I know I have to be like butter. In order to be like butter, I have to forgive." I sat and cried with my son as he wept in my arms. We all had to make that choice every day in order to make it through this storm. As a family, we made the decision to be like butter. It was one of many times we had to make a conscious decision to forgive so that we could stay strong and thrive in the most difficult of situations.

Ron – Forgiveness Even in Despair

In 1993, my accuser, now a young man, recanted his testimony. He admitted that he had lied; I knew I was going home! It was finally going to be over. As soon as I got the news, I began to go through the 2 foot by 4 foot lock box that held all of my possessions. I held each item and thought about which inmate in this place could most use this stuff since I would not be needing it any more. I took my treasures out one by one; my sweat suit, my shorts, my headphones, the cassette tapes I had listened to so many dark nights, my Bible (this I decided I would keep), books, letters, and cards. I carefully sorted out the personal items that I would take with me and placed them at the very bottom of the locker box. I couldn't wait to give the rest of the items away! I decided that as soon as I received word that I was riding back to the county for my hearing, I would distribute the rest of my belongings to the men in here who would appreciate the gifts. Weeks passed before I received the news I had been waiting for. I had a hearing! The night before I rode out, I gathered together with the men who had kept me focused and encouraged me to become better. We ate together and encouraged each other for what we believed was the last time inside the gates. As I rode out early the next morning, I stared at the stars in the sky. It was the first time in 2 years that I had seen the stars. How could I have taken their beauty for granted all those years when I could have seen them every night and seldom looked up? They were stunning against the dark night sky, and seemed to twinkle just for me to see. I imagined my sons and my wife looking out their windows and seeing the same stars, and then let myself daydream about what it would be like to be home with them again.

The next day was the hearing. As I arrived at the courthouse, Joe, my attorney, met me with a somber look on his face. Joe had been volunteering his time on my case since my conviction and I knew the look on his face meant bad news. My heart sank; something was definitely wrong. The first words out of Joe's mouth were, "Ron, I am sorry to tell you that Aaron, your accuser, called the judge last night to revoke his recantation."

"What?! NO! This cannot be happening," I thought to myself. I looked around trying to decide how to process that news. Nothing this tragic

FRIENDSHIP

FAITHFULNESS

FORGIVENESS

FAIRNESS

FORTITUDE

happens to someone twice! I simply could not believe that this man would tell another lie; but it was happening. I went into the courtroom and sat through that heart breaking day. My accuser admitted he had lied at the trial and that he had actually been using drugs right before he testified against me. However, he now wavered and did not completely revoke all of his testimony. I was devastated. He had been warned the day before that he could be charged with perjury and sent to jail if he said he lied on the stand. I knew he wanted to tell the truth so we could both be free, but he lacked the courage to do it when faced with the consequences for his actions. I instantly knew what this would mean for me; I was going back to prison to serve out my sentence.

Anger and resentment began to creep back in. As I returned to prison and had to face everyone I had said good-bye to just the week before, bitterness filled my heart. Later that night, I lay on my bunk and began to scream, "Why, why, why, Lord?" I felt a tug on my heart and opened my Bible to find an answer for the pain that was overtaking me. God admonished Job with the words: "Where were you when I formed the heavens?" I read in astonishment. "Oh, Lord, I am so sorry. You do not owe me an explanation!" I knew in my heart God was looking for an answer from me. "I was with you, Lord. Your word says that You knew me before the foundation of the earth." Peace came over me as the Lord spoke into my heart and said, "I still have you."

"Asking for and receiving forgiveness makes offering forgiveness so much easier."

I chose to forgive, again and again and again. Forgiveness, I had learned, was not a single gesture. Bitterness constantly knocked on the door of my emotions, telling me I had the right to invite him in. Truly, it became easier to forgive others after I experienced forgiveness in my own life. It is so easy to concentrate on how terrible others are when you ignore your own mistakes and sin. It is funny how we hold grudges against others and ignore our own shortcomings and wrongs. Asking for and receiving forgiveness makes offering forgiveness so much easier.

Cathy – The Hardest Forgiveness of All

It was December 2001 and we were in another hearing requesting Ron's release. There was a light covering of snow on the ground, but the air was fresh and crisp and invigorating – not bone chilling like it can be sometimes in Ohio. As we walked into the courtroom, I kept praying, "Please Lord, let it be today. Let my husband come home to us today." It had been over 10 years since he had gone to prison. Life was different; we were different. The only constant was our love for each other and our family. And even that was not a constant; it had grown over the past 10 years into something stronger than I had ever imagined it could be. When the judge walked into the courtroom, we all rose and then waited for the bailiff to grant us permission to sit. As he began to speak, I knew there was something different this time. He was looking at us intently. As each attorney presented their case and arguments, my heart began to beat faster. I just knew a miracle was in the air. As the judge began to speak, an expectant silence filled the air. He said he knew Ron had been maintaining his innocence for the past decade, but he also knew Ron had not lived an exemplary life before going to prison. He asked Ron what he had learned during his time in prison.

Ron stood up and told the judge that the one thing he had learned was that the only thing a man truly owned was his word. Everything else could be taken from him - his possessions, reputation, family, everything. He went on to tell the judge that more than anything else he wanted to instill that lesson in his sons, to help them become men of their word. Ten minutes later, the judge released Ron! I was in shock. All these years I had waited, prayed, and hoped for Ron's release from prison and here it was. Ron was free! I picked him up from the county jail, still in his prison uniform. It was like a dream come true! Our first Christmas together in over a decade was the greatest gift we could have ever hoped to receive. We wept and held each other saying over and over, "You are home. You are home. You are home." It was beautiful; it was the answer to our prayers.

Six months later, I was three months pregnant and we were so happy that our beautiful family was growing. We were unloading groceries and the phone rang. As I picked up the phone, our attorney said, "Cathy, I am so sorry. The court of appeals has overturned Ron's release. That is all the information I have. I do not know how or when for sure, but Ron must return to prison." My mind went blank and I began weeping. Surely this could not really be happening – we didn't even know it had been a possibility! How many times do we have to walk through the valley of injustice and despair?

Ron put the phone to his ear. As he heard the news, he turned to look at the expectant faces of his two sons who were now teenagers. One tear rolled down his face as he looked at their frightened eyes. Later, as we sat down to ponder what to do next, Ron looked at each of his sons and then grabbed them and they wept together. When the attorney called back, he informed us that the judge had given Ron one week to turn himself in to the county jail to be transported back to prison.

One week. It felt like a death sentence. I never cried so much in my life. I begged and pleaded and bargained with God, trying to find a way to stop this from happening to my family again. I watched as my sons' eyes grew dim and veiled with pain. We spent the week at a camp-ground playing, fishing, crying, and talking together. The week sped by and then it was time for Ron to go back to prison. Our last morning together, as we prepared to take Ron back to jail, I watched 15-year-old Blake stop crying and begin to build a wall around his heart. I watched 13-year-old Brandon square his shoulders and lose the light in his eyes. I stood there looking at Ron and wondering how on earth I was going to live through this day, not even thinking of all the days past this one. Ron grabbed me and pulled me close to him and kissed me through my tears. He held me so fiercely I thought he might never let go. Then, without warning, I felt him leave me emotionally. I felt him withdraw into himself and detach from us as he prepared to go back into that world. I knew he needed every ounce of strength he had in order to do what he was about to do. But it didn't change the fact that I felt aban-doned as he removed himself from me. I cannot remember a time since becoming a Christian that I felt so alone.

As I watched my husband walk back into prison, I felt a mixture of grief and pride. Pride in watching my husband do the hardest thing I could imagine anyone ever doing; walking back into prison to serve time for a crime he never committed. He walked in with his head held high, with honor and courage. But he left us behind grieving the loss once again. I went home and wrapped myself in his towel, laid my head on his pillow and breathed in the smell of him. I thought I would never wash that pillowcase. Then, just a few nights later, I reached over for his pillow and pulled it close to me. As I pushed my face into the pillow, I couldn't smell Ron anymore; all I could smell was my own shampoo. I wept for the loss of the last part of Ron in our home. Bitterness swelled back up inside of me. All of this pain, all of this loss because of one person's need to have an excuse for their behavior. I struggled for weeks with the bitterness and pain.

> *"Practice does not make perfect; it makes permanent."*

We had to go back to our 3 hour visits and 5 second embraces in the prison visiting rooms. It was tortuous to see him here again. Our sons were shutting down emotionally, and I was completely overwhelmed as I stood trying to hold our family together, pregnant and alone in society again.

Once again, we had every excuse for refusing to forgive. We could hang onto our bitterness and be completely justified. Our story could have been told like this: "Once upon a time, there was a happy family that was torn apart by a grave injustice and they never recovered. They became angry and bitter and lived the rest of their lives in misery because of this injustice. Everyone felt sorry for them and agreed with them that they should be angry and bitter and not ever forgive the people who had robbed them of the life they should have had." But that is NOT our story; thank the Lord! That is not our story.

We decided to tell our story the way it should be told. We were determined to have a happy life and a happy ending. You see, we had learned that a story cannot end happily unless happiness is woven all through the story. You don't live your entire life miserably and then all of sudden live happily ever after. We chose to forgive. We celebrated the gift of the baby I was carrying and the gift of the 6 months we had experienced together as a family. It was a painfully sweet reminder of what it was like to be together; we focused on the sweet part so we could endure the pain. We did this one day at a time. Forgiveness is a choice. Sometimes it is one you must make over and over and over again - but it still is a choice that you must make.

Ron – Practice Makes Permanent

Forgiveness is something that must be constantly practiced in your life and relationships. Practice does not make perfect; it makes permanent. Our marriage is not perfect, and our family is not perfect. But it is healthy, and it is permanent. My relationships with my wife and children are permanent because we work at them every day. Healthy relationships are made that way by forgiveness. Bitterness will cause a relationship to sicken and die. People who remain bitter and angry believe that it is a choice that will only affect them, but the reality is that everyone around them suffers because of it. Their spouse and children lose the opportunity to be part of a healthy, strong relationship, and they miss out on all the wonderful benefits of moving deeper in commitment and love as they navigate through conflict together. Marriage is full of disappointments and opportunities for conflict, hurt and pain, but that only makes it the perfect place to practice forgiveness! Building a strong marriage requires practicing forgiveness every day. Without mastering forgiveness, it is impossible to master any of the rest of the High Five principles that build a strong marriage and family.

Ron – It is Hard to Forgive the Little Things Too

Frequently it is the little things that cause rifts in a marriage or relationship. Surprisingly, in our work we see more relationships torn apart by small offenses than by a single, large offense. After spending 15 years in prison and finding forgiveness in the midst of being imprisoned, coming home and learning to live together as a family was more of a challenge than I expected. I was surprised to find that although we had learned to deal with big issues, the small ones were the ones that created the biggest potential for rifts to be formed.

When I was released permanently in 2006, I moved back home and into life with my family. I began to create some space for myself, literally, moving things out of Cathy's closet to make room for my things. While she was gone one day, I carefully arranged the closet so both her things and my things would fit in the small space. I folded her "extra" clothes and put them in boxes under our bed. I took all of the stuff I considered unimportant like letters, cards and storage boxes out of the closet and put them in another room. I was so pleased with the work I had accomplished and how I had made room for both of us in one small closet. I imagined how pleased Cathy would be when she arrived and saw all of our stuff hanging in the closet together! As Cathy arrived home, I greeted her and enthusiastically shared with her that I had a wonderful surprise for her. I led her to our room and opened the closet door with excitement. Then, I stood back and admired my hard work while I waited for the praise I was sure would be lavished upon me. To my surprise, there was a long silence. Too long. Uh-oh, something was wrong. I looked over at Cathy and saw the set of her jaw and the flame in her eyes. She was upset, and I mean REALLY upset! I was incredulous. How could she possibly be upset?

"Where are the rest of my clothes and all my keepsakes?" she demanded.

"Under the bed and in the loft," I said hesitantly.

"What? Why would you take my things out of my closet and box them up? There is not enough room in this closet for your things! This is MY closet. Why would you do such a thing?"

I was utterly speechless. In my mind, what I heard her say was, "There is

no room for YOU in my life." I quietly began to take my clothes out of the closet, HER closet, and take them to another room. She was still furious with me for not talking with her about moving her clothes out of the closet before I did it. I was hurt and feeling very unappreciated and unwanted.

Anger began to build up inside of me. She was rejecting me and my help. I began to think about all the things I was trying to do for my family and started feeling resentment toward her for treating me this way! We each pulled back our emotional connection from each other and this further fed our anger. As I went up to the spare bedroom, I seriously contemplated whether I should just move all of my things up there and make that my room! She obviously did not want to share her space – maybe even her life – with me. As I hung the clothes in the large closet upstairs, a thought occurred to me. WE could move upstairs. Not I, we. Hmmm … an idea began to form in my mind of how I could use this as an opportunity to connect us instead of widening the chasm that it was creating.

As I went downstairs to talk with Cathy about my idea, I found her crying as she was sorting through the things I had boxed up and put under our bed. I watched her and it dawned on me that it wasn't just about me. Her whole life had been turned upside down again. She had been the one managing all the chaos and navigating through all the social discrimination while I had been away. The closet was the only place that was just hers; everything else in her life was freely shared. I had violated the only privacy she had. Everything about our lives was public; she opened our home and cooked for all the neighborhood children. She worked hard to help me through the past 15 years, and I had just taken the little place she had reserved for herself, a tiny little closet full of her clothes, keepsakes, and memories. Oh, was she still angry! She looked up at me and I knew I was in big trouble. (I cannot tell you how happy I was that I had figured out WHY she was mad at me!)

In that moment, it struck me that we had just weathered 15 years of trauma together, and here we were fighting over closet space; yes, closet space. I apologized to her for invading her personal space and her closet and asked her forgiveness. She just stared at me and I knew it would take some time for her to settle down and offer forgiveness for my intrusion. I chose to forgive her and not take it personally. It would have been really easy to keep feeding my own rejection, telling myself it was all about me and what I wanted or needed. A reaction like that was not going to help us grow closer or resolve this issue. I chose to look for a solution that would work for both of us and cause us to connect in an even deeper way. Later that night, I shared with her my idea of moving our bedroom upstairs and adding a new closet so that we would each have our own large closet. She loved the idea. We talked about why she was so angry with me and what we should have done differently. In the end, we each forgave each other. Learning to let go of the offenses and embrace the freedom that comes from releasing others is what had given us the ability to move beyond the hurt for the past 15 years. It is also what keeps us thriving every day together as a family now. Practice makes permanent, and practicing forgiveness helps your family become healthy and permanent.

Brandon – The Journey of Forgiveness

When I first started working with my parents, I realized that I had a lot of bitterness built up in my heart that I had not dealt with. As we began speaking, writing and traveling a lot together, I began to discover all these things that I thought I had dealt with. I never realized how mad I was that I never got to experience having a dad to play with as a child. Emotionally, I was stuck. I kept trying to figure out a way that my dad could play Legos or army men with me, but every time we tried, it just felt forced. I remember driving in my car, feeling extremely angry, thinking that my childhood had been robbed from me. I called one of my close friends and told him what I was feeling and thinking, and he said, "Brandon, would you rather have had your dad while you were growing up and not have him now or accept the fact that you didn't have your dad home while you were a child, but now you and your dad have an amazing relationship and enjoy each other?" I said, "Naturally I want him now, but it still hurts knowing that I will never know what it's like

FRIENDSHIP

FAITHFULNESS

FORGIVENESS

FAIRNESS

FORTITUDE

playing games or learning things with my dad as a kid." He said, "Of course it's going to hurt, but holding on to the pain is not going to help you heal. You can either refuse to forgive your dad for not being there for you as a child, harden your heart and not have a relationship with him now, or you can forgive him for not being there, and embrace the fact that he is here now while you are an adult."

Whenever I talk to this friend I always feel stupid because he sees right through the complicated mess and makes the solution seem simple. It is really easy for me to blow a situation way out of proportion, but really the answers are easy. Either you can forgive and let go, or you can cut off the relationship. I realized I wanted the relationship, but I still wanted to hold onto the pain and bitterness that I thought I was entitled to feel. The more I learned about the details of how my dad was taken from me, the more anger and bitterness I felt. But once I started to forgive, each step became easier to take. The journey had begun, and I made the decision to practice forgiveness.

Ron – Forgiveness is a Choice

The truth is that if you are bitter at someone, you cannot maintain a healthy relationship with him or her. Bitterness is an indicator that your relationship is in critical condition and needs immediate attention. When a relationship is weakened by bitterness and anger, time will not heal it because all the problems just sit there waiting for you and will worsen while they are neglected. Everyone experiences pain and disappointment in their lives and relationships. In every family, there is both joy and pain. What we do with that pain is our choice. It is a conscious decision to forgive those who cause us pain. For some, it is difficult to forgive even an inconvenience. We can get so focused on our own needs and what we want, and then when we do not get our way, we become angry and resentful. Things, events, or people that move us away from what we want can become the focus of our anger. If we do not forgive the actions of others, or sometimes their lack of action, then anger plows the ground in preparation for bitterness to grow. Once bitterness has taken root, relationships suffer. Is anything more important than those you love? Are you ready to embrace forgiveness as a natural part of your relationships? We are not talking about staying in destructive or abusive relationships or living in denial; the answer is not merely enduring an unhealthy relationship. We are talking about actually walking in forgiveness and rebuilding the trust which builds a healthy marriage and bonds a family together. We are talking about the redemption and reconciliation that is possible for any relationship.

Cathy and Bria – "Monkey See, Monkey Do"

"Slow down. Turn right here. Watch out for the curb. Watch out for the car next to you. Slower!" The instructions came out of my mouth even though I knew that with each one we were getting closer to an argument. One of the worst habits I had was "helping" Ron drive. I really began with the best of intentions; I am frequently his navigator and I want to do the best job possible. So, I would give him step by step instructions. All the while, Ron would get increasingly irritated, and we would inevitably have a disagreement. After months of this cycle, I began to feel very convicted about being the proverbial "backseat driver." I was determined to stop telling him how to drive. I decided the best way to do this was to keep myself occupied while I was in the car until I had broken this habit.

As we prepared for a two hour car ride, I selected a book to read. The trip began wonderfully! I took my book out and began to read. I did not say one word to Ron about his driving, and I was feeling so proud of myself. Bria was 5 years old at the time and riding in the back, right behind Ron. "Papa, slow down! Papa, you are going too fast. Papa! There is a car coming!" I listened to her repeatedly shouting instructions at her father. I laid my book in my lap and looked at her. "Bria, stop telling Papa how to drive. It is not your job to tell him how to drive." She innocently looked back at me and stated, "I know. It is yours, but you aren't doing it!"

Our children pick up on our attitudes and behaviors, and it influences their belief systems. When we model forgiveness, so will they. Nothing is as wonderful as seeing a child forgive fully, from the heart; no adult can hold a candle to it. The High Five must be modeled, not just taught.

FRIENDSHIP

FAITHFULNESS

FORGIVENESS

FAIRNESS

FORTITUDE

Practice Makes Permanent

In order to keep yourself accountable in your progress toward strengthening your family, you must ask yourself these questions:

⌒ What am I spending my emotional energy on?

⌒ Who do I hold unforgiveness toward and how is it affecting my family?

⌒ Do I allow problems and disappointments to come between me and my spouse, or do we work as a team to solve them?

⌒ Who do I need to forgive so I can live my life free from bitterness?

There is nothing that is worth carrying bitterness around for. No hurt, betrayal, or loss is worth the damage that unforgiveness will create within you and your relationships. Allowing yourself to judge the actions of others only poisons your own heart. Learning to forgive is key to building a strong, healthy family. Without the ability to forgive, we create an emotional vacuum that can never be filled. We live our lives in constant turmoil and spend our energy seeking revenge. Make a commitment to practice forgiveness and model it for your spouse and your children. It is a selfless act that requires diligence to practice, but it is an act that will always build and strengthen your family.

Learn to practice forgiveness in your life using these simple steps:

✎ Write a list of people you need to forgive. Every day as you wake up, remind yourself you are forgiving them. Every night, pray for those people and say the words out loud, "I forgive you, _____." When you are at peace in your heart toward your loved one, erase them from the list or tear up the paper. Make time to talk to the person you have been holding unforgiveness against and tell them you forgive them. If you cannot meet with them, write a letter and send it to them, but follow up with a phone call. There is no substitute for talking with someone.

✎ Write a list of people you need to ask to forgive you. Set a date on your calendar for each one and label them "FREEDOM" and add an initial of their name. On this day, you will call or meet with them to ask for forgiveness. Absolutely NO TEXTING or E-MAILING on this one. In order to restore a relationship, face to face is always best. If the person lives far away, a phone call is the next best thing. As a last resort, write a letter, but remember you must follow up with a phone call or face to face visit as soon as you can. No one said this is going to be easy, but we promise you it will be worth the effort. Remember, asking for the forgiveness is all you have to do. It is not your job to convince them to forgive you.

✎ For future offenses that threaten your relationships, as soon as you realize you are carrying an offense, mark your calendar for the day you will lay it down and forgive the offender. Write RELEASE DATE on your calendar on that day. Do not set the date any further away than a week. This will allow you time to have your emotions calm down, talk through it and balance your emotions with reason. Look for ways that you contributed to the situation that caused the offense. If, after you have forgiven the other person, you find that you still feel angry, mark a new date on your calendar that you are going to completely forgive. Let go of the past and look forward into the future. Redirect that energy into something positive.

With this ring,
I thee wed

Cathy and Brandon

Ron and Brandon

Cathy, Blake, and Brandon

Brandon, Cathy, and Blake

Family photo during 1st release

Brandon
and
Bria

prison   visits   with   dad

Christmas without dad

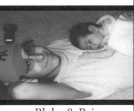

Blake & Bria

Halloween

Brandon, Ron, and Cathy

Blake

Brandon and Blake

prison

visits

with

dad

Blake and Brandon

Blake, Brandon, and Bria

Brandon

99

Bria and Cathy

Tijerina Family

Brandon,
Ron,
and Blake

Blake, Ron, and Brandon

Ron and Bria

Blake, Bria, and Brandon

Fairness – Learning to see in our circumstances the opportunity to use effective communication skills to resolve conflict and strengthen our relationships

Ron – Fairness vs. Justice

At some point in our lives, we have all said, "This is not fair!" When I was sentenced to serve a prison term for a crime I did not commit, that is what my heart cried out. It is what the hearts of my family cried out. But the truth is that life is full of situations and circumstances that seem unfair. No one ever gets what they think they deserve; at least not here on earth. We all think we are entitled to the best that life has to offer, but that is not at all what we truly deserve. Justice means receiving what we REALLY deserve. If we receive anything good at all, it is not because we deserve it! There is a season of joy and a season of pain in every human being's life. Practicing fairness means looking for the good result that can come from the pain we experience in our lives. We just need to choose to have the proper response to those circumstances. Sometimes the inconveniences or offenses we experience are like a pop quiz; they are opportunities to test our response time. Do we do what is right and take this opportunity to make the choices that will build up our family, or do we get hung up in the wrong response to the situation? Success does not come from WHAT we receive; it comes from what we DO with what we have received.

The High Five principles have the power to transform your life and bring healing to your family. Few people have lived through the trials that we did, and yet we stand, and with us stand the thousands of families whose lives have been changed by applying these principles.

When you are in the midst of a situation that seems unjust or unfair, it is difficult to see past your circumstances to the larger picture, and the larger purpose behind the pain and inconvenience. When others seem to have more than their fair share of good things, or when we seem to have more than our fair share of bad things, that is when we need to practice fairness the most. It is true that we frequently learn more from our mistakes than we do from our successes, and we also build our families stronger as a result of the difficult circumstances and pain in our lives than we do when things are easy and fun. Our family learned that it is also possible to have joy in the midst of unhappiness. That joy and peace came from knowing that what we were doing and how we were treating one another was right.

Comparing our circumstances to those around us can create a sense of loss and an attitude of powerlessness. If we give in to these feelings, we will begin to live as if we are victims. In this way we become little more than mere characters in another person's story, and not the authors of our own stories.

Thankfully, we don't have to live this way, consumed by envy. Our sense of fairness needs to be properly calibrated so that we can experience gratefulness for every good thing we have, and gratefulness for the things we do not have as well. I cannot control the material blessings that other people enjoy that I seem to lack. Envy is about wanting things that properly belong to another; having those things in our life is beyond our control. But fairness is completely within our own control. We have the power to enter into a new and richer understanding of fairness for our family. We had to make the decision that we were going to view our life story as an opportunity to build family strength. As you join us on our journey to discover the true meaning of fairness and how it is part of building a strong family, think about your own viewpoint and experiences and how you want your family to experience fairness.

> *Comparing our circumstances to those around us can create a sense of loss and an attitude of powerlessness.*

Brandon – Learning to "Play Fair"

"Life isn't fair." We've all said those words when things didn't go the way we thought they should. Being raised in a single parent home wasn't fair. Having to go to several different prisons all over the state of Ohio to see my dad wasn't fair. Feeling like I couldn't talk about my dad around other people wasn't fair. The list goes on and on. So what? What does that mean about my life, my value and my perspective on the future? Is fairness an important ingredient to a happy, successful life? Absolutely! The next question, then, is how can we properly respond to a seemingly unfair or disadvantaged life situation?

I have never heard a parent say, "Today I had to teach my kid how to NOT share their toys with other kids.

Responding properly to the things that we can't control is probably one of the hardest things to do. Is it because we are selfish and want everything to go as we plan? Yes, of course that's why! We are selfish people. I have never heard a parent say, "Today I had to teach my kid how to NOT share their toys with other kids. I wish they would just become more selfish and think about themselves more often!" That is completely ridiculous. We naturally want everything for ourselves and have to constantly remind ourselves to play fair, think about someone else first, or share something we want to keep for ourselves.

I have a niece and a nephew, whom I love so much. My niece is five years old and my nephew is three. I also have a nine year old little sister whom I love. (She will tell you I love to torment her - actually, I do!) I do so because I love her.

Almost every weekend my parents take my niece and nephew to spend the night at "Grandma and Grandpa's house." They all get along for a couple hours, but then my sister and niece get tired of playing with Dawson, who is one of the busiest kids I've ever met, and they start to be mean to him. One day my parents and I were in the kitchen downstairs talking when suddenly we heard my nephew crying and knocking on a door and yelling, "Hey, let me in!" My parents asked me to go see what's wrong. It never fails; the girls had locked him out of the room and were playing with their dolls, completely ignoring him. The crazy thing about this situation is that when the door was finally opened, my sister and niece had a fort built and all their dolls laid out in a row. They were peacefully playing and enjoying their toys. It's as if they never heard my nephew banging on the door yelling at them to let him in so he could enjoy playing too.

That is how I felt about my life while my dad was in prion. During the day I acted like nothing was wrong. I smiled, laughed and played with friends, but once my world got quiet and I was alone with my thoughts, I would be yelling in my head, "Just let him come home!" Almost every night I would ask, "What did I do to deserve this type of pain and heartache? Why won't my mom's family stop fighting my dad? When will this chapter of life end?" I would ask those questions until I cried myself to sleep.

Since none of those questions were being answered, my solution was to turn to a dream world. Since living with both parents at home was clearly not going to happen for me in the real world, I began to wish. "I wish my dad was home. I wish my family wasn't poor. I wish. I wish. I wish." After a while, I realized how stupid that was. I began to pray and really try to figure out why this was happening to me.

As teenagers, my brother and I were pretty nice to each other and generally played fair. We knew how to share and get along with each other since most of the time that was all we had. Every once in a while something would happen that would rattle the cage of testosterone we each had inside us. We would get mad at each other for no reason, or I would do something that would irritate Blake to the point of no return. I don't really know why I did that to him, but apparently it seemed like a good idea at the time.

I especially remember two times when I was really mean to Blake and it caused him to react. I used to go into his room across the hallway and just start stomping on the floor, singing super loud, playing with his things and being as generally annoying as I could. One day, in my normal routine of irritating my brother, he warned me to stop picking on him, but I kept doing it. After about ten minutes of pure irritation, he jumped at me and we started wrestling. I don't remember what exactly happened, but I do remember him taking it too far and hitting me in the face. Immediately we both stopped and looked at each other. Then suddenly Blake started crying and ran to his room. I stood there completely confused, thinking, "Wait a minute! I'm the one who just got punched in the face. Why is he the one crying?" After I calmed down, I went upstairs to his room and asked him why he was crying. He said, "Because when Mom gets home, you're going to tell on me, and I'm going to be the one who gets in trouble." After he said that, we both starting laughing and then everything was fine.

> When we think about others first and have consideration for them and choose to respond to our situations in a way that strengthens our relationships, then we are practicing fairness.

Another time, we had a friend over and we were having a championship competition on Nintendo 64. We were playing one of the Madden football games, and I was playing against Blake. He has always been a lot better than me at sports games, and I passionately hate losing, but I still played against him. The first half wasn't too bad for me. I wasn't behind by that much and I felt like I might be able to catch up, but I felt that anger inside of me starting to get bigger. The second half started, and I couldn't catch up to his score in the third quarter. The fourth quarter was almost done and there was no chance of me winning, so instead of playing fair and letting him win I took my controller and threw it at him. It hit him in the face, and both my brother and friend stared at me while I stormed out of the room extremely mad. I got grounded from video games for a couple weeks after that.

I failed that particular pop quiz.

What does fairness mean? We all want things to go the way we want. The moment we encounter some type of resistance from our friends, family, or the world, we frequently react according to our biased opinion of how we think the situation should turn out. We often let our selfishness control us and we become focused on ourselves instead of thinking about the whole picture. When we let those feelings turn into selfish actions, then it becomes a problem. How can we change our way of thinking? We need to ask ourselves, "What makes my plans more

important than other peoples' plans? And how will my response to this situation impact others?" When we think about others first and have consideration for them and choose to respond to our situations in a way that strengthens our relationships, then we are practicing fairness. Choosing the proper response to a family situation always strengthens a family and shows others that you love them. That is the opposite of selfishness.

Brandon - Learning Not to Fight Your Circumstances

Like my father, I was a professional musician. When I was in a band, I had to learn to go with the flow, and I had to learn it fast. We would practice our set list and plan out how and when we were going to switch songs, do jumps and guitar throws, but it never failed; invariably something would happen. Either the computer would crash or the sound system would fail. The stage would be too small, or we would be rushed and not have a sound check. We would all feel frustrated and "take it personally." I would usually think to myself, "How could they do this to us? Don't they know who we are?"

The funny thing is that we were an indie band, and of course they didn't know who we were. The sound man had been at his venue all day, listening to music he probably didn't even like, and most bands we played with thought that the louder they were, the better they sounded.

In those situations, there was nothing I could do to change what was happening. I had two options. I could throw a fit, say that it wasn't fair, refuse to play and walk off the stage. Alternatively, I could go with the flow, not take other peoples' seemingly unjust moods and attitudes personally, adapt to the situation and play the best I could. Most of the time I chose the second option, but I'm willing to admit that there were times when I let my frustration affect my attitude, and that always affected my performance.

Learning to go with the flow is not something most people can do easily, but once you learn to let go of your agenda and lose your self-focused mentality, then you will be a better life performer. No one can perform well when they are trying to change things that are beyond their control. Once I calmed down and thought about how other peoples' days were going, I realized that my desire to over-control was a symptom that I was being selfish. When I recognized that, I had the power to just go with the flow, practice fairness and use my creativity to find a way to move forward.

Cathy – Fairness Means Considering the Other Person First

After being gone more than a decade, there was that day when Ron was suddenly released from prison to come home. It was a wonderful, joyful, long awaited day that we had prayed for! My sons had been 2 and 4 when their father went to prison for a crime he never committed. It had been a long road filled with many opportunities for us to witness God's faithfulness in various areas of our lives. Now, we had a wonderful opportunity to celebrate the beginning of a new season – and I thought it was the end of the season of separation. My husband was home; my children finally had their Daddy home. What a beautiful day!

It is so amazing to me that we often pray about only what we want and never stop to think about praying beyond that moment in time when heaven opens its gates and we finally get what we have been praying for! From the moment Ron walked out of the prison gates, I could not imagine what else I could ever want now that I had my family back together. I sat across from Ron and just stared at him. It was so wonderful to watch him just BE with us; to look up and see him smile at me across the room. As every moment passed my heart was filled with increased joy and my eyes with tears. I had not fully realized how much I had missed his presence in our home. The house felt warmer, fuller, and complete again. All the little things we had been practicing in our relationship and family made the transition smooth. Our family was strong and healthy. The years of practicing being a healthy family during the incarceration had made us a permanent healthy family. Our family had more than survived - we had thrived through all those years of prison visits, phone calls and letters. Even so, we were unknowingly heading for an event that would remind us that even in healthy families, there is conflict.

FRIENDSHIP
FAITHFULNESS
FORGIVENESS
FAIRNESS
FORTITUDE

After Ron's return, it did not take long for a confrontation to arise between him and our oldest son, Blake. The second day he was home, Ron went to sit at the head of the dining room table. Blake was sitting in that seat, at the head of the table. Ron casually told Blake that was his place and Blake could move to sit next to him. Blake didn't budge, he insisted this was HIS place and Ron could sit next to him. Ron gently but firmly told Blake, "I'm home now. This is my chair." Not wanting a confrontation, I immediately stepped in and told Blake to move. As we had dinner, Ron talked about all the things he planned to do that evening around the house. Blake quickly ate his food, and asked to be excused. Ron finished his meal, and we lingered at the table just enjoying being together again. After dinner, Ron went to take care of the chores he had talked about over the meal. Much to his surprise, he discovered that Blake had run ahead of him and done everything. I looked over at Blake who was sitting nonchalantly on the sofa with his headphones on and a book in his lap. "Thank you, Blake," I said. He just looked at me and shrugged his shoulders. I could see the message he had sent: "We don't need you." I wondered if Ron saw it too.

The next night, as Ron came to the table, there was Blake – back at the head of the table. He sat there stubbornly staring ahead, almost daring Ron to challenge his right to be in that seat. As I watched them, I knew I could not interfere again tonight so I stepped out of the dining room and into the kitchen. Ron reminded Blake that his seat was on the side of the table. Blake did not respond, and it was obvious he was prepared to go to battle over this symbol of headship. Ron reached out and touched Blake's shoulder. Blake flinched. He did not turn his head to look at Ron, but he held his fist clenched close to him; he was ready to fight for what he believed belonged to him. I said a small prayer and bit my lip to keep from saying anything. Ron spoke calmly. "Blake, I am home now. You don't have to carry this heavy load alone anymore. You get to just be the son. It's OK, Blake, I am home. I have you." Blake blinked and swallowed hard. Then, as I held my breath and waited to see what he would do, he relaxed his clenched hand and quietly got up and moved to another seat. Blake did not say a word, but he never again sat at the head of the table at our home.

> It isn't always easy to be fair to someone and consider their concerns in the midst of a disagreement.

This scenario could have ended so differently. If Ron had decided to assert his authority and simply insist that Blake submit and move, there would have been a fight in my home that night. Who knows how long that rift would have kept Blake and Ron locked in a power struggle? Thankfully, Ron chose to use the situation to connect with Blake and acknowledge Blake's pain and internal turmoil rather than dismiss his feelings as unimportant or invalid. It was an amazing moment in our family's life. That confrontation began to build the bridge between my son and his father that had been wasting away in a broken heart for over ten years. It isn't always easy to be fair to someone and consider their concerns in the midst of a disagreement. It is, however, the most effective way to build connections between two people at odds.

Ron – Resolving Conflict with Fairness

Within days of my first homecoming, Blake and I had several confrontations. I saw the look of hurt and pain he tried to conceal deep inside of him. He thought I couldn't hear him crying out in grief over all the years we had lost. He was so good at masking his pain with sarcastic humor that he had fooled most people into believing he was managing very well. Soon after we had the confrontation over the seat at the table, another confrontation presented itself. This time, I couldn't easily defuse the anger and pain that had been bottled up for so long. I asked Blake to help me take the trash out, and he ignored me. I asked him again and touched his arm when he wouldn't look at me. He jerked away and ran up to his room. I followed him and stood in the door watching him. I could see he was about to release some of his anger. I said, "Blake, I am your father. I am home now, but I know it has been a really difficult time for you."

He stood up and came at me swinging and yelling, "You might be my father, but you will never be my Dad again. Do you hear me? I AM NOT LETTING YOU IN MY LIFE!" I grabbed him to keep him from hurting me and held him close while he screamed and cried. "You will leave me again. I know you will. You might die or go back to prison or just leave. I cannot live through losing you again, so I am not letting you in! I can't let you be my dad again because you can't promise something won't happen to take you away from me again. You can try all you want, but I am not letting you in!"

Although I was holding a fourteen year old in my arms, I heard the four year old Blake yelling at me for suddenly leaving him and missing out on an entire decade of his life. Tears welled up in my eyes, and it took all I had to not sob with him. I was still holding Blake tightly, and he was sobbing and fighting against me. Slowly he relaxed and his sobs quieted. I loosened my hold, but he stayed in my arms with his head on my shoulder softly hiccupping. My poor son. He had convinced himself he had to shut out the world to keep from getting hurt. He had hardened his heart to protect himself from the hurt of being abandoned and living a nightmare. I was at a loss for words.

He was right. If I promised him I would never leave him again and something happened, the pain would be worse. On the other hand he was also wrong. He wasn't being fair to himself or to me. Risk is an inherent part of every relationship. If you are going to be close to someone, you will get hurt; if it isn't by an action or word, it will be by death since no person escapes dying. Death usually takes us one at a time and someone is left hurting and alone. I had no way of knowing what the future held.

> When I am not here beside you, God is. He is always here.

So I agreed with Blake. "You are so right, Blake. I cannot promise I will never leave you. I do not know what the future holds for either of us. I can only promise I will never leave you on purpose. You are also very wrong. I am more than just your father, I am your Dad. I will always be your dad whether I am here beside you or not. When I am not here beside you, God is. He is always here. God is the only one who will never leave you, never forsake you and never let you down. Trust God, Blake. Unimaginable as it is to me, He loves you more than I do, and He knows you better than I do and will carry you when I cannot." God had taught us that no matter how many people live in your house, or what their earthly relationship to us is, His role as Father has to be recognized as the most important in every family. Life is full of things that are not fair. In order to be fair to Blake, I had to tell him the truth. He was right, but that is not what he wanted to hear. He wanted me to promise him I would be there forever. It would have been easy to just make the promise; but it would not have been the fair thing to do. Little did we know how important that lesson was at that time. Six months later, the court overturned my release, and I had to walk back into prison. Although Blake deeply grieved, he did not have the pain of a lie and broken promise to bear on top of the separation. Fairness does not mean giving someone what they think they want, or what you think they deserve; it means being honest and considering the impact of what you say or do, not just in that moment, but for their future growth.

> "I sat in the waiting room, pregnant, overtaken with grief, and angry. I was wondering how this could possibly be fair."

Cathy – Practicing Fairness for the Sake of Others

When you feel like the whole world is treating you unfairly, it is hard to treat others with fairness. When Ron returned to prison, I felt so victimized. We had done everything we knew to do in order to live responsibly and honor our faith in God. Yet here we were, separated from each other again. It took every ounce of bravery I had to go back to visiting Ron in prison again. Both Blake and Brandon were completely devastated and kept telling me they were not going to go back to a prison visiting room. However, they somehow mustered the courage to visit their father and went with me.

The reluctance wasn't just about not wanting to be reminded of the pain of being apart, it was also about the experience of feeling like a criminal

FRIENDSHIP

FAITHFULNESS

FORGIVENESS

FAIRNESS

FORTITUDE

by default. As we walked into the reception area and took our number, we sat in a huddle with about a dozen other families also waiting to see their loved ones. The chairs were lined up in rows and there were signs posted everywhere with the rules for visiting, the laws about taking contraband into the prison and various warnings about behaviors that could get us kicked out of the visit or arrested. I sat in the waiting room, pregnant, overtaken with grief, and angry. I was wondering how this could possibly be fair.

We processed through the line, and we were ushered into a visiting room already overcrowded with families. As we came in, other families had to terminate their visits to make room for us. It was gut-wrenching to watch the disappointment on their faces as the guard called their names and informed them their visit was over. The moms gathered up their crying children and pulled them toward the door as we stood silently watching their visit end so ours could begin. One of the children turned to see who had just robbed her of her precious time with her father. She found us standing, waiting for our table and gave us a vicious look that cut right to my heart. I knew her pain at having her time cut short with her Daddy. I didn't want to steal from her the scarce moments she had to hold her Daddy's hand and look into his eyes for the comfort she desperately needed. I gave her a sad smile and nod, hoping she would understand that I wasn't deliberately taking him away from her. Her disappointment and anger turned to tears as she followed her mom out the door.

I wanted to leave. At that moment, I wanted to take my two teenage sons by the hand and take them somewhere we could hear laughter instead of crying; somewhere it was fun to be instead of painful. I wanted this agony to end more for them than for me.

We were seated in a back corner near the vending machines around a small, square black table. Just as we sat down, I saw Ron emerge from one of the doorways on the side of the room dressed in a brown jumpsuit. He looked tired. A deep, weary tiredness had settled on his brow. He put on his best smile and came to greet us. We held each other closely for our full 5 seconds and then pulled away before we were chastised for too long of an embrace (at that time in the prison visiting room a couple could only hug for 5 seconds). We looked at each other without saying anything. None of us could think of a thing to say. Here we were back in a prison visiting room when we were supposed to be home together. This nightmare was supposed to be over. I could not bear the heavy silence, so as cheerfully as I could, I asked, "So how are you, Ron?" but I choked on his name and began to sob. As hard as I tried, I could not hold back the tears. We all began to cry together. There we were, sitting in a crowded room, not talking at all; just sitting there, holding hands in our little circle and crying. Ron began to pray the prayer we had been praying together for 12 years. "Thank you, Lord, for our family. Thank you for taking care of them when I cannot. Lord, use us to bring glory to your name; send us where no one else will go."

I snapped my head up at that point. If this is what it looked like to live out that prayer, then I was done. I was not going to live my life "going where no one else would go." I boldly proclaimed, "I just cannot do this anymore. This is not fair. I cannot bear it, and our sons cannot bear the pain either." Ron just looked at me through his own tears and asked me, "So what does that mean? What will you do instead of this?"

His question startled me. What would I do instead of this? What else was there to do? I stared defiantly back at him, refusing to answer his questions. "I would live happily ever after with my husband home and my sons healthy and HAPPY," I thought to myself. That option, however, was not available to me. I only had two options: fight to keep my family healthy and together or give up. I could not give up and still have my family together. I needed to look outside of my own pain and see what I could do to help my family navigate through these rough waters. I had been so preoccupied with sitting in my own self-pity that I had not even considered what I could say or do to lessen the pain for my family. Ron's question struck something deep in me and reminded me that I had a higher call to answer. I was called to lead my children. If I did not choose to live fairly and justly in spite of the chaos around me, I would be giving my children victimized lives. Fairness is not about getting

what we think we deserve or want. It is about treating people in our lives with concern and compassion even when we don't get our own way.

Ron – Recalibrating the Scale of Fairness

"Fairness." I didn't even want to think about that word as they processed me back into prison. The six months I had just spent with my family seemed like a weekend furlough. "Do men who get to embrace their wives, eat with their families and tuck their children into their beds at night know how blessed they are?" I knew in my heart they did not. They were out there, taking for granted all of the gifts of freedom, and I was sitting here in a prison cell longing to be home. As the clerk was completing my paperwork, I noticed that I was being processed as if I had violated parole. I pointed out to the clerk that this information was not correct. Without even looking up at me, he informed me I would have to write a letter to the central office to request that an investigation be done to change my status. Until then, I would be processed as either re-offending or violating parole. On top of everything else, this was the breaking point. It might seem like a small point but at that moment I wanted to scream, "THIS IS NOT FAIR!" But I just kept moving through the process of entering back into the system. Visions of my expectant wife and two broken-hearted sons kept flashing through my mind as I put one foot in front of the other.

Finally I arrived at my new cell in the Corrections Receiving Center. Dressed in a brown jumpsuit once again, I fought back the anger that swelled inside of me. It was a constant battle against the tide of anger rising up and then falling back in my heart. Just when I thought I could settle my emotions to endure the coming days, months or years so that I might serve in a purposeful manner, anger would rush in with an overpowering sense of unfairness. I cannot tell you how many times in those days and weeks I had to choke back the anger that arose out of the unfairness of my circumstances. The suffering that my family was experiencing was desperately unfair. All of our friends went back to living their normal lives, but not my family. My children and my wife felt abandoned once again. The abandonment was multiplied this time because we were living our lives honestly and responsibly before the court of appeals overturned my release. I began to resent those who were not suffering as I was. The sense of unfairness and belief that I had been robbed of the life I was entitled to was eroding my sense of purpose and my ability to connect with my family in order to help them navigate this season of our lives. I knew what was happening, but I felt like I was in a losing battle. Thoughts of giving up and resigning myself to the inevitability that I could never have a healthy, happy, normal family life kept sneaking in to further discourage me. The environment I was in was draining me of what little strength of will I had on reserve.

No matter what anyone tells you, in prison, your life is on the line every day. One mistaken word or action and people are beaten or stabbed. It happened every day. Part of me was tired of doing all the right things just to experience more injustice. I was at my lowest point since coming to know the Lord.

The next morning, I saw my name on the mail list. I stood in line to get my mail and hoped it was from my wife. I missed her desperately. My life felt empty without the sound of her laughter, the smell of her hair and the sight of her gleaming, joyful green eyes. I thought of our unborn child and prayed this baby would be strong and healthy. I would miss the experience of feeling my child move in Cathy's belly and the joy of seeing her born. It bothered me that someone else would take my place at Cathy's side and hold my child before I would even know she had been born. My heart ached. I pushed thoughts of her away because they were too painful. I needed to be on my guard as I cautiously began to build new friendships inside these dangerous walls. The cadence of, "This is not fair," played over and over in my mind, feeding my anger and pain. I shut down my emotions as I went to pick up my first letter.

To my surprise, it was not just one letter. I had received 7 letters! Each letter was from a different person. I held the letters in my hands and fought back the tears. I do not even know how to explain the feeling of being remembered in the midst of the most difficult circumstance of your life. I was not forgotten. People cared about me; about us. I decided to save my wife's letter for last. I would open her letter that evening so I could be alone and savor the moments with her uninterrupted. I read all the other cards and letters. Hope began to spring up in me. Story after story about how my experience was impacting others was in those letters, along with words of encouragement and prayers. I began to feel the heaviness lifting off of me. I thought about my family and hoped that they were also receiving this outpouring of love and life.

Later that evening, I opened my wife's letter. Her letter started with, "My beloved husband, hurry home." A stab of pain ran through me. She of all people knew if it were in my power, I would be home. I could feel her pain and loneliness in her greeting. I read her letter, which was encouraging me to stay strong and updating me on all the things that were happening on the outside in my family's life. I could also read between the lines and see that she was struggling. She was battling in her heart and mind. She was struggling with the unfairness of my return to prison. I began to ask myself what I could do to help bring balance back to her life. To rescue my family from unfairness, I realized I had to throw off my own feelings of victimization and do everything I could to focus on helping my family see that I was all right so they could be all right as well. I needed to focus all my attention on investing in our family to create a stable family experience that would be so unique to us that it would balance out the loss we had to endure. It was our only chance to make it out of this together. I had to level the playing ground by doing all I could to exhibit fairness toward my family.

Fairness in our Family

From that time on, fairness took on a whole new definition for us. Fairness meant examining our actions and determining if what we were doing was bringing strength to our family or causing more pain. Were we considering the wants, needs and feelings of those we loved, or were we stuck in our selfishness? Could we change our perception of our circumstances and create an aroma of fairness so that each member of our family felt considered, included and valued? I knew we had to internalize fairness in order to experience it. If we spent our lives focused on our selfishness or our expectations, we would forever be the victims of the loss we had suffered. On the other hand, if we could practice fairness by using those circumstances to focus on each other's experiences and feelings, use our communication to resolve conflict and build each other up, then we would be able to bring hope and strength to our family regardless of the difficult things that might come. Fairness became my encouragement, as I began to weigh out my actions and words on a scale of fairness that measured my commitment to my family's success rather than my entitlement to have what others had.

Cathy and Bria – Going Barefoot

Bria was going to be late, and wasn't happy about it. We had just moved into our new home. We had been here for three days, and finding our things in the piles of boxes was quite an adventure. "Mom! Papa! I can't be late! I don't like to be the last kid in the class!" Bria yelled.

It was the end of her second year at a new school, and she was finally making new friends just as summer was approaching. "Bria, come on! We are loading the car," Ron yelled up the stairs as he walked out with 2 computers and a backpack.

I was desperately searching for my hairbrush. Bria came bounding down the staircase with a brush in one hand and her shoes in the other. "I found them!" she exclaimed. "Good! Hurry, Bria. I made you a breakfast burrito to eat on the way there. We have to leave right now, or you will be late," I told her.

She grabbed her burrito and ran out to the car as I brushed my hair quickly. I ran out to the car and jumped in as Ron backed out of the garage. We all breathed a sigh of relief. We had made it! Bria would be on time, even with the 20 minute drive to the school. Bria was eating her breakfast and happily chatting with us about all the fun activities they would be doing at the end of the school year.

As we turned onto the school road, Bria suddenly exclaimed, "I forgot my shoes!"

"No, you didn't, Bria. Don't tease. I saw you with them," I chided her.

"No, REALLY. I forgot my shoes! I laid them down to pick up the food, and I never picked them back up!" she explained.

"WHAT? Oh, no!" I said. We all burst into laughter. Bria laughed until she fell over in the back seat. "Well, Bria, we don't have time to go back home and get them and still get you to school on time. Just go to school without your shoes and we will bring them to you." She stopped laughing, and for about 10 seconds she thought about this news.

"OK. But hurry, please. If you are fast, maybe no one will notice!" Ron got out of the car, opened her door, and escorted his brave, barefoot daughter into the school. He let the secretary know we would be back soon with shoes for her. Thankfully we found her a pair of shoes at the store next to the school and took them over to the school secretary who promised to get them to Bria as soon as possible.

After school, Bria came running to our car with a huge smile. "You will never guess what happened today. Before you came back with my shoes, we had a fire drill, and all the kids who went out the door with me noticed I didn't have any shoes on." She shared with a twinkle in her eye.

"How did you feel?" I asked her.

"Well, after a few minutes, I decided not to be embarrassed. I told them that my teacher said I made history today! I was the first child in the history of the school to show up without shoes."

> *"The choice to embrace the moments of our lives and respond with fairness is ours alone to make."*

We have the opportunity, with every challenge, to make history in our family. We are writing the blueprints for our children and our grand-children to build their own families. The choice to embrace the moments of our lives and respond with fairness is ours alone to make. We can react in anger and frustration when things do not go our way, or we can take the opportunity to learn and grow stronger and healthier.

Practice Makes Permanent

⌒ When you are in a situation that you feel is unfair, do you look for the hidden opportunity to strengthen your family through the proper response to the situation?

⌒ Do you consider the experiences and feelings of others first?

⌒ Do you look for ways to be grateful even in the most difficult circumstances in life?

⌒ Do you seek to resolve conflict lovingly, considering the other person and their position, and looking for ways that you are responsible or have contributed to the conflict?

Maximize fairness in your family by following these three steps:

- On a sheet of paper, make 2 columns. Write down the times you have felt treated unfairly or dishonored in the left column. Make a box on the bottom of the left column and list the action(s) or words that were unfair below it. In the right column, list what you would have wanted your loved one to say or do.

- On a separate sheet of paper, make 2 columns again. List the times you have been unfair to a loved one in the left column. In the right column, list an alternative that you should have done or said instead.

Share this with your spouse or loved one. Be honest.

 FRIENDSHIP

FAITHFULNESS

FORGIVENESS

FAIRNESS

FORTITUDE

✎ Have a conversation with your spouse about a time you felt dishonored or treated unfairly. Allow ample time for each of you to communicate your feelings openly and collaborate with your spouse to make a plan for how you will practice fairness in the future by considering the other person first and weighing the impact of your words and actions.

We highly recommend taking the Couple Communication I and Couple Communication II courses by Drs. Sherod and Phyllis Miller to help sharpen your communication skills. This program took our communication and relationships to the next level. If you are serious about building quality communication and effective conflict resolution skills with others, this program is a must.

*Fortitude – The strength of mind, will and purpose
that enables a family to courageously face danger
and endure pain or adversity together.*

Strength to Finish the Race

I once heard a man say, "No great thing is ever achieved through average means." As each of us works toward attaining the things that we have dreamed of having, strength is needed to finish the course. Fortitude is the strength to stand on your convictions and do what you know is right even in the face of inconvenience, pain, adversity, or danger.

In a physical body, strength is what makes us capable of meeting the challenges of our environment and resisting the attacks of disease. Strength is necessary to create and sustain life. Building a healthy family takes work; and this kind of work requires emotional strength. Strength takes time to develop, and there are different areas where it is required. There is strength to meet the challenges of outside forces that tend to separate and destroy the family, as well as the internal strength to do the things necessary to promote trust and encourage sharing. Strength of mind involves knowing what is right; strength of will is deciding to do what is right; and strength of purpose is holding firmly to that larger good that brings meaning to your actions. All three combine to produce fortitude.

These strengths are developed by all the things that we do to prevent or heal the attacks on the health of our family. Practicing the High Fives requires courage, and that courage comes from the commitment to the higher good of building the health of your family. Sharing the deepest parts of yourself in order to build your friendships, remaining faithful in the face of temptation, forgiving offenses, asking forgiveness for your own failings, and looking past your own expectations in order to extend fairness to others – these all require fortitude. You have to be willing to do it even when the work is inconvenient or unpleasant, remembering that the work will bring growth and greater strength. Sharing honestly creates friendships; faithfulness creates the trust that is vital to solidify friendships and help them to grow; forgiveness will heal wounds and open up the possibility of reconciliation and potentially even greater levels of sharing and meaning in your friendships. Extending fairness to others allows friendships to survive the hardest of trials. Fortitude, then, is consistently choosing to do the little things that matter and having the proper response to your circumstances, even when you do not feel like it. As fortitude grows, it creates the ability to stand your ground in the face of danger.

FRIENDSHIP

FAITHFULNESS

FORGIVENESS

FAIRNESS

FORTITUDE

Fortitude is also about meeting the challenges of an outside force that is determined to harm. It is facing fear with a determination to not let it master you. It means recognizing danger when it is present and becoming the shield and defense for the other members of the family. You do not have to look for outside adversaries; they are all around. The family is under attack in ways that are unparalleled in, perhaps, all of history. Those attacks are evident in the messages, the media, and the harmful people your family is exposed to; there are destructive forces that the family needs to be protected from. Making a commitment to protect and defend those in the family who are the most vulnerable, especially your children, is essential in keeping your family intact and strong.

> *Fortitude is also about meeting the challenges of an outside force that is determined to harm.*

Keep in mind that even in the midst of the worst pain, no matter what, you must find a way to keep standing. Your children are watching everything you do and hearing everything you are saying. When I was told I was going back to prison and had been given a week to turn myself in, my whole world went crazy. I wanted to run as fast as I could and never look back, but I knew I couldn't. Every lesson and every test I had gone through in prison had been in preparation for this moment in my life. Nobody ever said to me that doing the right thing was going to be easy. I knew that whatever choice I made, it would permanently impact the lives of my children, and it would forever set the course of their lives. A father wants nothing more than to see his children become better people than he could ever be, and I knew I never wanted to see Blake and Brandon go to prison or end up struggling to make it. I remember telling them as we all cried, "Boys, you must always remember that the right thing is always the right thing, no matter what. Your dad has to do the right thing."

> *Fortitude is a discipline. A discipline is developed the same way muscles are developed, by trials to the point of exhaustion.*

Fortitude is a discipline. A discipline is developed the same way muscles are developed, by trials to the point of exhaustion. As muscles recover from the most extreme workout, they rebuild themselves and become stronger than they were before. The next time they are worked, it takes longer to exhaust them. But when a muscle is not worked to exhaustion, it is not an effective workout. Feeling the burn in your muscles is like feeling the pain in your fortitude; it means that you will be stronger next time you get a workout. If you do not work hard on the discipline of fortitude, you will be weak instead of strong, and unable to even keep standing.

Ron – Fortitude is Standing Your Ground in the Face of Danger

After I was convicted I was sent to Lucasville Prison where I was to serve my time, I was brought into the prison to be processed. We were lined up against a wall and one of the corrections officers (C.O.s) who brought us here began taking off our shackles. After he finished, we were told to strip down and walk over to the table when our number was called. After about six or seven guys were called, I heard my number, which was 250-397. I walked over to the table and I received three sets of shirts, underwear, and socks. I was told to get dressed. At the next table I received toothpaste, a toothbrush, a razor, bed sheets, a pillow case, a blanket, three blue shirts and three blue pairs of pants. We were then asked our shoe size and were given pairs of shoes and a laundry bag. I was told to finish getting dressed and put everything else in the bag. After everyone was dressed and packed up, we stood there waiting to move out. The captain gave us our welcoming speech. He told us that if we acted like men, we would be treated like men, and if we acted like animals, we would be treated like animals. He then told us he was going to give us a towel before he showed us to our units. As we all followed the captain, we entered into a brightly lit hallway. We were in E-complex, and had just come from the quarter master. Here we had the length of our pants hemmed to fit us properly. When they were done, he then took us to see the laundry room. He said that if we had clothes that we could not stand to lose, we should not send it down here to be washed. Nine times out of ten, you would not get it back, he told us. Next, he took us to the printing shop; this is where most of the paper that is used in the offices in Ohio prisons is printed. Then he took us to the shoe factory; this is where all the state shoes for all Ohio prisons are made. These two factories are called Ohio Penal Industries (O.P.I.). As we went into these places all eyes were on us. Of all the men that I saw working in those shops, not one was smiling. Everyone's face was hard and cold.

I really didn't know what to make of what I was seeing. The shock of me being here was still fresh. I kept replaying in my mind all the stories I had heard about this place. (Lucasville had notoriety as the toughest and most dangerous prison in Ohio.) Then I started praying, "Lord, please protect me; do not let me get attacked, and do not let me get raped."

We were then told we would be leaving E-complex and going to our housing unit, and on the way there, we would see the rest of the prison. As we walked down the hallway, we passed a long corridor. The Captain told us that this was the maintenance department, where later I would go to work as a machinist. Leaving E-complex, we had to go through a standing metal detector, a hand held metal detector, and a pat down. Next we all walked up to a gate and waited for a C.O. to give someone in a booth a signal to open it up. For the rest of my life I will remember the shrill cry of the gates opening and closing and the clicking sound of the doors being unlocked and then locked again.

We were then told the reason we were not issued winter coats. Every place we were allowed to go was inside, and in winter time, the recreation yard would be closed. I would not experience fresh air for months.

Finally, the gate opened, and we moved on. A few feet to our right was the med bay booth; this is where everyone who had to take medication would come for their pills. Next to that was the control booth that worked the two gates in this area, and another long corridor that led to the front of the prison and the visiting room. Right across from these booths and corridors were the two large dining halls, better known as the "chow-halls." One was for K-side, the other for L-side. The prison population was divided into two different sides [why K and L?]. Right past the chow hall by a few feet, we stood in front of the second gate. The C.O. who was leading us through the prison gave the signal to the C.O. in the booth to open the gate.

As we all began walking down the bright white hallway, a C.O. pointed out the two strips of yellow tape which ran all the way down the corridor. He said, "The middle lane is for the C.O.s. Stay in the outside lane in lines of two. If a C.O. sees you cross the yellow tape, you will receive a conduct report."

No one spoke as we walked on. All one could hear was the sound of our shoes hitting the floor. For a place housing more than fifteen hundred men, the silence was surreal. There was no yelling, no laughing, no talking, and no crying. All you could hear were gates opening and closing over the rhythmic sound of people walking.

We came upon a Y in the hallway. The hallway to our left and the one in front of us to the right were both blocked by gates. At this junction was a table, another metal detector, and a booth where a C.O. controlled both gates and monitored movement. Putting our property on the table, we all walked through the metal detector. The C.O. then called out our names followed by the announcement of who was going where. The hallway to our left was called the K-unit, and the other one was called the L-unit. Each side had 7 or 9 units or living quarters. I was told I was going to L-1.

FRIENDSHIP

FAITHFULNESS

FORGIVENESS

FAIRNESS

FORTITUDE

Approaching the gate, the C.O. gave the signal to open it up. Three or four other guys, the C.O., and I walked into the L-side. About one minute into our walk, we came to another gate. The C.O. told us that on the other side of the gate was where we would be living. I felt my heart beating faster and fear gripping my body, causing me to sweat, but I felt cold. I told myself, "Stay strong, you can do this, stay firm." As I am writing these words, the fear that flowed in me then is so real now that I am reliving it. I know had it not been for the power of the Holy Spirit, I would not be telling my story today.

The C.O. on the intercom told the control booth to open the gate. The final gate was coming open. I said another prayer. "Please, Jesus, cover me. Protect me. Do not let anything happen to me, please, in Jesus' name. Amen."

We walked through and L-1, the unit to which I was assigned, was directly to our left. I was the only one in our group assigned here. I felt I had to keep moving, but my legs were shaking. Every prison story I have ever heard, every prison movie I had ever seen came rushing into my mind. I kept telling myself, "Keep your head up. Do not look down. Do not let them see your fear, and whatever you do, do not let them see you cry."

The C.O. knocked on the door and another C.O. from inside came and opened the door. Peering in from the hallway, it looked like I was going into a tunnel. It was dark and gray, the lighting an off-white yellow color, which made it look like nighttime even though it was still noon. As soon as I entered, I could hear people talking, music playing, and the sound of automatic doors opening and closing. It appeared that we were on a platform that looked out into the length and depth of a long galley. Seeing the C.O.'s control console in the center of the platform, it looked to me like the inside of an ancient slave galley ship that was propelled by the men in the cells, with the C.O. as the one yelling, "Row! Row!"

One of the C.O.s working his unit asked me for my name and number.

I told him, "Tijerina, 250-397." He then told me what cell I would be going to. I cannot remember the number; it was on the first floor about ten cells down, forty feet from the C.O.'s control station. Walking off of the platform, I went down about five steps to the cement floor of the ancient galley. As I looked around, I felt my breathing become fast and labored. My eyes were wide open, and I tried to take everything in. I kept telling myself to keep moving and look like I have done this before. I felt like I was seeing my surroundings through the eyes of a child; everything looked enormous in size.

As I walked toward the cell, I saw someone above me on the second floor, I thought to myself, "This is crazy! They have women here, locked up with men." As the person came more into the light, I could see it was a man trying to look like a woman. I then cried out within myself, "Oh God, where am I?"

Walking by the cells, some men were looking at me, and some paid no attention. I could feel the eyes of the men staring at me, wondering what cell I was going to. Nothing in my life had prepared me for what I have already gone through nor for what I was about to face. I wanted to keep my gaze straight ahead, but I couldn't. I had to look for the number of my cell, so I had to look at each one of them.

Each cell had bars on the side of the door and a hole in the wall. The door itself had a little window opening. Through the bars I could see a set of bunk beds, a desk, a chest with drawers, a sink, and a toilet. Everything was cold metal. At the end of each cell there was a window to the outside. Some men were watching T.V., some were playing cards, and some were just watching me find my way. As far as I could see, there were two men per cell. The walls were a green turquoise color. The paint was flaky.

I felt like I was walking down a plank getting ready to plunge into shark infested waters. I found myself standing in front of my cell. I saw a black man sitting on the bottom bed watching a TV that was on the desk. He turned to look at me and I nodded my head as a greeting. He

FRIENDSHIP

FAITHFULNESS

FORGIVENESS

FAIRNESS

FORTITUDE

turned back to watch his TV. I then turned to look back toward the platform, which looked like it was a mile away. The C.O. working the control panel saw I had found my sarcophagus in the wall and the door automatically began to open, making a low pitched humming sound, similar to the sound of the gates in the hallways.

I entered into the cell and, seeing that the top bunk was vacant, I set my belongings on it. I introduced myself as TJ. The man stood up, we shook hands, and he said his name was "Bill" and that they called him "Crazy Bill." I later found out why. He was a little taller than me and about forty-five years old. He told me he had been here in Lucasville for the past ten years. After this initial introduction he did not speak to me anymore. Since I was unaccustomed to prison life and didn't know my new social culture in this terrible place, the silent treatment unnerved me.

I had been living with Bill for a week, with no privacy, even for my bathroom needs. Because of this, I had not wanted to spend the time it would naturally take to have bowel movement. It wasn't that I did not have to go, but rather, being too nervous, I wanted to avoid sharing this private act with my new roommate. I had been going to the chow hall for three meals a day for a week, though, and finally my stomach could not take it anymore. Being locked in the cell most of the day, I had seen Bill hang a towel over the bars for privacy when he had to relieve himself. The pain in my stomach had become unbearable; I had no choice.

When I was in the county jail and on my way to prison, I had met men who had been there before. They told me about some of the things to watch out for, but they forgot to tell me one thing: When you are sitting on a toilet in a prison, take one leg out of your pants and place it on the floor . . . If your space is intruded, you don't want to find that your pants are acting as an ankle cuff that will entangle you and keep you from being able to protect yourself.

My top priority at that moment was to find relief from my discomfort,

"Lord, protect me and give me strength." so I jumped off the top bunk, telling myself, "I can do this." I hooked up the towel the way I had seen Bill do it. A few minutes later, Bill actually spoke. Not since the first day that I arrived had he said more than two words to me, and now he decided to speak. He said to me, "You owe me!"

I could not believe what I was hearing. I said to myself, "Jesus, help me!" I gave Bill a stern look and trying to show no fear, said, "What, man? What did you just say?" He then said, "You owe me for watching my TV and living in my cell!" I could not believe what I was hearing. I began to pray within my spirit saying, "Lord, protect me and give me strength." Then I said to Bill, "Let me take care of my business and then we will talk about this." I turned my back to him to pick up the toilet paper and when I came up, BAM! He hit me on my right temple with his fist. I knew I was not only fighting for my manhood, but also for my very life! I know it was only by the grace of God that I fought him off. I came back at him with all my strength and he gave up. When it was over, I had the imprint of three bars on my forehead, both my eyes were black and blue, and my nose was bleeding and felt like it was broken. My teeth felt like they were going to fall out and both my lips were busted open. Though I did not see it until later, despite my having been beaten, I had the victory. At the time, all I could think about with enormous relief was that my greatest fear had nearly, but not in fact, come upon me.

When it was over, I must have been in a state of shock, because I did not call for the C.O. right away. It was not till the cell door came open again, about an hour later, that I went up to a C.O. to tell him what had happened. I really did not have a choice but to explain the fight, given the way I looked. After telling them what happened, they took both of us to "the hole" for fighting.

In prison, when a person gets in trouble, depending on the severity of his offense, he can be sent to what is called "the hole." It is a more secure type of lock-up, used to separate those who break the rules from those who are more cooperative. These cells typically had a sink, toilet, bed,

FRIENDSHIP

FAITHFULNESS

FORGIVENESS

FAIRNESS

FORTITUDE

and shower, so there was no leaving once put in one. You got to walk outside once a week, if that, and your food was delivered. A stay there could last between one day and two years.

I was found guilty for fighting and stayed there for one week. During this time of isolation, I cried out to God. "Why, Lord? Why did I have to go through that?" It was not until after I was let out of the hole and sent back to the rest of the population that I came to understand a little of the "why." By fighting Bill and prevailing, I had not only earned the respect of the men, but I had set a precedent for myself, showing that I was a man and I would fight. In the fifteen years of living in this world, that was the only time I was tested in this manner. After six days, I got out of the hole, and a captain approached me to ask me if I thought my life was being threatened. If so, I could check myself in to protective custody, which really meant going back to the hole.

Because I knew a little about running a millwright and a lathe, I had been given a job working in the Maintenance Department as a machinist. I was busy at work when the boss and one of the welders, another convict by the name of Yusef, came up to me and asked how I was doing. I told them I was okay, but that I was considering the offer to go back into the hole for protective custody. They both were quick to say, "Don't do it!" They told me I did not need to do that because everybody already knew what had happened, what Bill had tried to do to me, and that I had successfully fought him off. I took their advice and told the captain, "Thanks, but no thanks." The same day, I was told I was moving to L-3, two units over.

Brandon – Running the Race with Fortitude

It doesn't seem like my life while I was growing up would produce strength. It seemed like the sort of life that would produce weakness. My dad was in prison, my mom was on welfare, we lived in a trailer that was falling apart, and to top it all off, both sides of our extended family HATED each other. If that was all you knew about me, it would certainly seem like my life would be full of weaknesses, pain, and fear.

However, instead of using all of these things as an excuse to fail, our family embraced the habit of fortitude, which is the strength of mind that enables a person to encounter danger or bear pain or adversity with courage. We made it one of our virtues to live by.

I was eight years old when I figured out that people were looking at me differently. Neighborhood kids would ask me, "Where's your dad?" I would tell them, "Well, my dad is in prison." They would look at me like I was the reason he was in there. At the time I really took that personally. I would replay the situation in my head over and over again. What if I would have just said something else instead? What if I would have lied and said he was gone doing something really great? No matter how many times I was asked that question, though, I would always tell the truth, and then later I would wonder, "What if … What if?"

Eventually it wasn't as much of an issue because my brother and I were known as the kids of a convict. Since people already knew who we were, it was easy to figure out who our true friends were as opposed to those who were nice to our faces, but made fun of us behind our backs, or those who looked at us like a "project" to be worked on.

> "I am living proof that just because we are hurt or broken doesn't mean we can't run the race to win."

Every single morning I woke up and told myself that I wasn't going to let the pain of having a parent in prison stop me from enjoying life and being part of a loving family. It was the hardest thing I have ever done. I looked at myself in the mirror and said, "You can do this." I was not even aware of what I was really doing at that age; I was just trying to make it through another day of broken dreams with a broken heart. Now I understand why I went through it all. I had to feel the pain of having a parent in prison, living in a single parent home, overcoming the stereotype of being a child of an inmate, being the poor kid, and having to help my mom work so we could pay bills. It is because of that pain I had to endure that I am now able to help and relate to so many people who are going through the same things. I am living proof that just because we are hurt or broken doesn't mean we can't run the race to win.

My family has had so many people tell us that there was no way we were going to make it through my dad's prison term. We were told were going to fall apart, either while he was in prison or when he got out. People said that it was easy for my dad to be the nice guy while he wasn't living with us. They said that he wasn't doing drugs and getting drunk all the time while he was locked up, but that once he got out and had his freedom again, then he'd forget all about what he put us through. They believed that someone like him, a man in prison, couldn't possibly change.

When I heard people saying things like that, it hurt. What bothered me most is that they were so unwilling to allow others to prove they had changed or would benefit from a second chance. What I've learned about the negative people in these types of situations is that in most cases, something has happened in their own lives over which they haven't experienced the needed forgiveness. They are living out their lives pretending they are whole. Not forgiving ourselves or others after making a mistake can be one of our heaviest burdens. If we are carrying that bitterness around with us everywhere we go, then of course we are not going to be able to win the race. I'm not saying you can't run well if you have pain or baggage; after all, that's what fortitude is all about - running and finishing the race despite pain. But, if you haven't released bitterness and found forgiveness for yourself and others, it will hinder any relationship you will ever take part in; your race will be long and hard.

When I hear the word fortitude, a few words come to mind: strength, safety, and meekness. I also envision a man standing watch over his house, making sure that nothing goes in or out without him allowing it. Even though my dad was in prison, he was able to give us that sense of security. My dad was strong for my mom when she felt like she couldn't go on. He would constantly encourage her and be a leader for her. I heard someone say a great leader is one who empowers others to do things and lets them have the credit, but steps forward when times get tough and makes the hard decisions to lead his people out of the trials and tribulations back to steady ground. When I felt like I couldn't continue to hope or dream that I would have a normal family, both my parents would tell me, "We are not forgotten. Someday God will restore the years that the locusts have eaten." I clung to that. I kept telling myself, "There has to be a reason why we are going through this!" When I would start to dream and hope for some change in our situation, it seemed like something else would happen; my dad's parole would be denied or an important relationship wouldn't work out. It seemed like no matter what, that I would end up feeling desolate, broken into a million pieces and like I had to put myself back together.

I suppose in a perfect world feeling alone and broken is something no child would ever have to feel. Being broken and having to put yourself back together, while trying to stay positive and hopeful all the time, is exhausting. All these calamities made me feel like whenever something good happened in my life that something else was waiting to come along and break me even worse than I was before. It took strength to keep going through these cycles.

In case it isn't obvious, walking into a prison visiting room to visit your dad is an experience that I never want my kids to go through. First you have to sign in. Then go through the metal detector, grab your car keys, belt, shoes and other items from the bowl, and then walk through doors that lock behind you. Then you go into the visiting room and wait. I did this in order to visit my hero. My hero was someone that no one on the other side of the gates approved of.

Every visit, my dad would walk into the visiting room with the biggest smile, and in that moment, it was like we were the only family in the room. It felt great just to be together, but it never mattered how awesome a visit started; I knew in the back of my mind how each visit was going to end. I would have to say goodbye and then leave the prison without my dad. But the pain of knowing how the visit was going to end completely left my mind the moment I saw my dad walk in to the visiting room. The pain immediately turned to joy. No matter what I was going through with school, girls, even my brother, none of it was in

my mind because I knew my dad was willing to help me carry the weight of my life. Even in a room full of people that have done some pretty messed up things I felt safe and secure. I knew my dad had our backs. Both of my parents are extremely strong people. I never once felt like I wasn't completely protected.

Watching the way my dad would protect us and even the way my brother would try to be the man of the house was extremely influential on me. I remember feeling the desire to be strong in order to be able to protect the other members of my family. So when it was just me and my mom going to the grocery store or to the mall, I was always thinking, "YES! Now is my chance to be the man." This first started when I was maybe ten or eleven. My mom and I would be walking through the store while shopping. Often we would walk down one of the aisles when some guy or another, who would say, "Hi," to her and try to engage her in conversation. As soon as something like this started, I would stare at the man, looking as mean as I could and letting him know what's up. It struck me how effective this was. The guys would always look at me with this puzzled expression on their face before turning and walking away. "Mission accomplished," I would say to myself as I smiled from ear to ear. I needed to feel that I was protecting my family too.

> *"Nothing could ever create the sense of pride and fulfillment that having healthy, lasting and engaging relationships with Ron and our children brings into my life."*

As a kid that young, I could not have defined what the word "fortitude" meant, but I didn't need to know the word because my dad, my mom, and my brother were showing me what it looked like. They had strength of mind and the ability to endure adversity with courage. By watching them and wanting to be like them, stepping into that role wasn't that hard.

Cathy – Fortitude Grows Even Through Pain

I think of all the difficult times that helped us grow stronger and closer as a family. We learned to keep the small things small and to use the big things to build our character bigger. Ron, our sons and I experienced so much pain, disappointment and heartache together as we walked through those 15 years. We grew closer and stronger because of the pain we experienced together. The disappointments caused us to recognize the value of ten minutes of togetherness. Practicing the High Fives propelled us into the work we do now. Our programs have received national recognition, our non-profit is thriving and the families we work with are experiencing transformation. But, none of those things could ever create the sense of pride and fulfillment that having healthy, lasting and engaging relationships with Ron and our children brings into my life. Nothing compares to the joy of seeing my family intact and experiencing life's challenges and opportunities with them.

Brandon – Fortitude Forged by His Parents' Strength

I was about eight years old when I came to the realization that I couldn't remember spending a birthday with my dad outside of prison. We lived in a singlewide trailer in the middle of nowhere surrounded by corn fields and had two neighbors that also lived in trailers next to ours. Our trailer was brown and had tires on top to keep the roof from blowing off. The inside looked just as bad as the outside, but my mom did what she could to hide the fact that our home was falling apart.

On my eighth birthday, I had a little party and invited some of my friends from church over to celebrate with me. We put the presents in the living room on top of the coffee table and ate my mom's homemade cake in the kitchen. If you walked through the kitchen, you would enter the toy room where we all played games. I remember sitting there at the head of the table, broken inside and fighting back the grief of growing up without my dad to witness the everyday moments of my life. For some reason it hit me; I didn't know if I was ever going to spend a birthday with my dad outside of a prison visiting room. I had to keep my composure because I was the kid who was always smiling and making people laugh. So I just held back the tears and acted like I was collected inside and enjoying my birthday party.

After we got done eating cake and ice cream, we moved into the living room where there were two couches and a love seat. The carpet had stains from being so old and the ceiling had stains from all the leaks. We all gathered around the coffee table filled with presents from everyone, and I began opening them. I saw a card that my dad had sent me. Every year, my dad would send me a card telling me how proud he was to be my dad and how sorry he was for not being there for me on my birthday, but this year was different. I opened the card, and out fell a piece of Juicy Fruit gum. I was so happy! I thought to myself, "Yes! My dad got me a real present!" I really cannot remember what other gifts I got that year, but I know my dad sent me a card with a piece of gum in it and that was all that mattered.

That night, after all my friends left and I was alone in my room on the bottom bunk bed, I just started crying. I was so hurt and felt so empty inside. I remember lying there yelling at God in my head asking, "Why are you allowing this to happen to me? What did I do to deserve this?" After I got done yelling and complaining about my life, I just started asking, "God, are you there? Do you remember me? Have you forgotten about me? Don't you like me?" Then I had peace; a peace that didn't really make sense. I suddenly just knew that God had a plan for my life, and this was just a season. God had not left me alone, and He would be there with me for this journey.

A couple of days later, we went to go see my dad so I could celebrate my birthday with him. I was both extremely happy and overwhelmingly sad at the same time. We got into the waiting room, took a number and waited with the other families for our number to be called so we could go through security and enter into the prison. After they called our number, we walked up and signed our name and wrote the inmate number of the person we wanted to visit on a sheet of paper. Once we got done signing in, we had to proceed through the security check. We emptied our pockets, pulled them inside out, took off our coats, belt and shoes. My mom would put her stuff in a basket to pass through the metal detector. Then we would each walk through the metal detector one at a time.

I was often scared that something would go wrong, and either they would not let us in to see my dad or they would arrest us for wearing the wrong things to the visit! Each time, I would hope and pray that everything was going to be OK and that we would get to see Dad, and it always was. After we got done with security, we would walk through doors that locked behind us. We waited between these two heavy, locked doors while another C.O. verified that we were allowed to enter the visiting room. When we finally got into the visiting room, we would have to wait in line again for the C.O. to check our pass and then tell us where to sit. The room sounded like a gym and looked like a cafeteria with really little tables. It had cement floors and the concrete walls and high ceilings dwarfed the small tables with chairs around them. In the back they had a room with an inmate tending to it where kids could go to play with toys or read books if their parents allowed them to go. Mine didn't let us go there very often. On the other side of the room were vending machines that sold pre-packaged food, pop, snacks, and candy bars. The food always tasted terrible, but the joy of sharing it with my dad overshadowed the stale taste of it. So I ate every bite.

Usually on a visit I would always get a personal pizza, so naturally, that is what I ate that day as well. We all sat around the table and talked about how things were and what I got for my birthday. When we all got done eating I got a chocolate hostess cake that I would share with my dad as a birthday cake. All of us were trying to make the best of the situation while I tried to pretend that this "party" was normal. My dad never stopped telling me that this was not normal, though. He was always telling me we should not be here, in a prison visiting room, celebrating my birthday and how sorry he was that I had to experience the inside of the prison to see him. I remember trying so hard not to cry because there were so many people around us, but no matter how hard I tried, I always ended up crying.

The only nice thing about crying was that my dad would start crying with me, and I knew he wanted to be home with me just as bad as I wanted him home. He would hold my hand and tell me no one could ever really keep him from me because we carried each other in our hearts everywhere we went. My mom and dad and brother all sang Happy Birthday to me and then we ate the dessert together, each of us having half of a cupcake. We cried until we couldn't cry anymore then we laughed. We would just start laughing and it felt like a weight was lifted off of my chest. Then we were able to really get into the spirit of celebrating my birthday, and I would be allowed to go up to the vending machines and choose anything I wanted. We made the best of the time we had left on the visit by laughing and sharing stories and jokes. We would talk about anything and everything and the time flew by. It was so wonderful to be a real family. Before we knew it, the guard was yelling, "Ten minutes!" and we knew our time together was coming to an end. We just looked at each other as the pain of the impending good-byes rose to the surface. The reality of knowing that we were going to leave this world where I had a dad and enter back into the other world where I was fatherless began to, once again, settle down upon me.

I kept thinking, "I hope there is a next time. I hope nothing happens to my dad before we can come back to see him again." Then, we all stood up to get our 5 second timed hugs while we were monitored by the visiting room C.O.s. We said, "See you next time," but it felt more like "Good-bye." The whole time, my dad repeatedly said, "It's OK, Brandon, I will be home soon."

"But not soon enough," I would think as I walked out of the prison. We left him behind waving and blowing kisses. "I need you now, Dad," I would think. But as we walked back out of the gates, it was time to put on my happy face again for the outside world – even then, I knew it was not OK to show people that you miss a parent who was in prison. But the thing that strikes me now is the ordinary, everyday strength it took for my family to do this over and over. It really was like exercise and it made us incredibly strong.

FRIENDSHIP
FAITHFULNESS
FORGIVENESS
FAIRNESS
FORTITUDE

Cathy and Bria – Weathering the Storm Together

Shortly after we moved to our new house, Bria announced that she had a bird's nest outside her bedroom window. She insisted that we come and see the amazing bird and her nest. We walked into her room and looked out of the tall window across from her bed.

She was right; there was a gray dove resting in her nest, carefully covering her eggs. Bria named the bird "Peace," and every day she stood at her window and checked on Peace and her nest. With close observation, Bria began to notice that on some days, Peace looked different than on other days. As she continued to watch the nest, she realized that two different birds were actually taking turns sitting on the eggs! One day, it began to storm. The rain came pouring down, and the wind was whipping through the trees. Nine-year old Bria was gravely concerned for the two birds and the nest. We went to her room to check on the small bird family. As we approached the window, we witnessed the most amazing thing. The father had returned to take his turn at the nest, but Peace refused to move off of the nest. The rain was beating down on both of them. The father was trying to move Peace, but could not convince her to get out of the way. The storm seemed intent on upsetting the nest and destroying the family inside. But the father dove was not about to abandon his family. He settled on top of Peace and opened his wings to cover her and the eggs in the nest. We could not tell how he was hanging on; the wind ruffled his feathers and the rain pummeled his small body, but he did not leave his post. When the rain finally passed and the wind began to die down, he moved his wings back against his body. Peace wiggled herself free and flew off while he took his turn keeping their eggs warm.

Three days later, the two doves hatched out of their shells, strong and healthy. "Momma," Bria observed, "if the father and mother had not protected them, they would not have made it through the storm, would they?"

Practice Makes Permanent

∽ When you face inconveniences or pain, do you look for the ways you can make your family stronger through loving communication and support of your family members?

∽ When you are scared or facing danger, do you remember the larger good outside of yourself that brings purpose and meaning to your actions?

∽ Do you look to that purpose to give you strength to make it through every challenge and stand on your convictions?

∽ Do you consistently do what is right, even when you do not want to?

Use these strategies to help your family transform difficulties into triumphs and build fortitude:

∽ With your family, write a "family platform" that your family will stand on when it faces adversity, pain or danger. These are the action steps that your family is committed to follow so that they will have success as a family and be made stronger. Post this list where everyone can see it. (Make this a fun event. Order pizza and create an environment that all can contribute.)

∽ Remember that, just like working a muscle to exhaustion, fortitude is made stronger when it is worked to exhaustion. Make a list of the adversities your family has faced with fortitude that have produced that exhaustion. Next, list how those obstacles have helped to make your family stronger. Intentionally encourage and validate each member of your family every day. Acknowledge and affirm them in their successes in their efforts in overcoming these obstacles.

〜 When a failure happens, see it as an opportunity to practice fortitude and help your family to learn from their failures.

> 〜 **Strength of mind** involves knowing what is right – review your "family platform"
> 〜 **Strength of will** is deciding to do what is right – reaffirm your family's commitment to their platform and the benefits that come from the proper response
> 〜 **Strength of purpose** is holding firmly to that larger good that brings meaning to your actions – affirm your family for their fortitude in the difficult trials they have lived through and remind them of the ways that their actions helped the family to grow.

〜 Connect with each member of your family once a week to ask if there is a difficult situation that they are facing. Choose a different day of the week for each member. This discipline will take practice. Connecting with them each week will create a sense of safety and support in their lives that will help them overcome any obstacle.

〜 Together with your family, set an anniversary date for your family to celebrate making it through all the obstacles over the past year. Celebrate on this day each year. This date is only for your family so it should not be on any other holiday. Mark it in the calendar as FAMILY DAY and celebrate it as your personal family holiday every year.

A Healthy Family is Like a Healthy Body

Healthy families are not perfect, but they are permanent. To build that permanence, you need practice, just like building the health of your body. A person can be transformed from unhealthy to healthy through learning which diet and exercise habits build health, making the everyday choices that build those habits, and practicing them over time, remembering the larger goals to keep them motivated. When you practice those things that build health in your body, you become full of energy and life. You can accomplish almost any task when you have the energy required to meet the challenges in life. Just because you are healthy, though, doesn't mean that you are perfect! Health isn't about perfection; a healthy person still sometimes gets tired, sick, or breaks a bone. If you are healthy, however, you are able to respond to sickness and broken bones with healing. Being healthy allows you to wake up in the morning filled with energy and enthusiasm.

> *Health isn't about perfection; a healthy person still sometimes gets tired, sick, or breaks a bone. If you are healthy, however, you are able to respond to sickness and broken bones with healing.*

The same is true for healthy families. Healthy families still encounters challenges and difficulties. They navigate through family disagreements and painful life circumstances. They remain committed to doing what is right, because it is the only thing that will keep the family together.

Cathy – The Phone Call

"Blake, grab those bags from your mom! Cathy, you don't need to carry the groceries. We can unload the van. Why don't you go inside and start packing?" Ron said. Excitement filled the air. Our first family vacation! I could hardly believe it; my family was finally together after spending more than ten years apart, and now we were going to have a real vacation, like a normal family. "No one deserves to be this happy!" I thought to myself. I felt like I was living in a dream. Ron was finally home and we were a real family; together, happy, and now going on vacation! I could hear the boys laughing and talking with their Dad as they worked together to unload all of the bags. What a beautiful sound. Ron had been home six months now, but it still seemed like a dream.

I skipped into the house and began to gather the things we would need on our trip. I paused to thank the Lord for the gift of my sons, my husband and this baby growing inside of me. I made my way through the clutter of grocery bags that were scattered across the kitchen floor and into the living room to begin packing our supplies.

"Brandon, please bring me the first aid kit!" I called out as I took inventory of the things we might need for our long weekend away. Brandon didn't respond so I got up and made my way through the maze in the kitchen, back to the medicine cabinet located in the laundry room. I paused at the garage door to watch my three guys. They were still unloading groceries and arranging our bags to be packed. I smiled to myself as I looked at all the stuff. The things seemed to multiply as they were moved out of the back of the van. I started toward them to see if they needed my assistance. Before I could get their attention, the phone began to ring. I quickly turned back and dashed into the house; two careful leaps and I was across all the obstacles on the floor. I picked up the cordless phone and pushed the talk button. "Hello," I answered breathlessly. "Cathy?" said a familiar male voice on the other end. "Yes! Hi, Eric, how are you?" I warmly greeted our appeals attorney. "Cathy, I am so sorry. I do not have good news." There was a pause before he continued. "The court of appeals has overturned Ron's release."

He spoke so quietly I could barely hear him. It was as if he were struggling to get the words out. "What does that mean, Eric?" I asked, speaking each word slowly as I fought the panic beginning to rise inside of me. His next words confirmed my worst fear. "Ron will have to return to prison." The flood gates broke; hysteria rose inside of me. I held the phone away from my ear and looked at it as if it were responsible for the words that had just come through it. I tried to find a way to process what I had just heard. I dropped the phone. It fell to the floor with a crash. I backed away from the offending instrument that had just delivered the news that shattered my life, again. I covered my face with my hands, and shaking my head back and forth, I yelled for my husband. "Ron!" I called out. I covered my face with my hands and whispered, "No. Please, please, please, no. Please NO!"

Ron, Blake and Brandon rushed into the house, tripping across all of the vacation supplies to find me standing in the middle of room, clutching my heart with one hand and covering my face with the other.

Ron – Bad News

We were just about finished unloading the groceries and other vacation supplies when I heard the phone ring and then a crash from inside. I paused, waiting for Cathy to say, "It's okay! I just dropped the phone," but she didn't. Instead, I heard her crying my name. A chill ran down my spine at the sound of that cry. Something was terribly wrong. I rushed into the house to find her standing in the middle of the living room with the phone lying on the floor. "Who died?" I wondered. I picked up the phone and realized someone was still on the other line.

"Hello? Who is this?" I asked. "Ron, this is Eric. I just received a phone call. I am sorry, but the court of appeals has overturned your release. I don't have any other details right now, but I do know you will have to return to prison to serve the remainder of your original sentence of 14-25 years." I stood there looking at Cathy who had now dropped to the floor crying. Numbness fell over me. "Thank you for calling us, Eric. Please let me know as soon as you find out anything else." I carefully replaced the receiver on the charging base and turned around to face my family.

"What? What, Dad? What?" begged our oldest son Blake.

Fear had replaced the joy on both of my sons' faces. "They have already been through so much," I thought to myself. "It is going to be okay, Blake. My appeal was just denied." I spoke calmly, but my heart was pounding with panic. "Your family needs you to be strong; do NOT panic," I told myself. Cathy was frozen in the middle of the room, crying into her hands. I walked over to her and gently pulled her into me, wrapping my arms securely around her. She pressed her face into my neck, wrapped her arms around me and sobbed against my chest. I held onto her as tightly as I could. I felt the tears welling up in my eyes. They ran freely down my face, off of my chin and dripped onto Cathy's face, mingling with her own tears. Blake and Brandon awkwardly stood watching us and wiping their own tears away. I pulled one arm free and extended it, inviting them into our embrace. They came, and we wept together in a huddle. "We are going to make it through this together. I promise we will make it, no matter what the future holds," I told my family, trying to bring reassurance to us all.

Cathy – Panic

The fear that washed over me was born out of experience. I had already lived the hardship of being a single mom raising 2 sons alone for more than 10 years. Now, here I was 3 months pregnant, and the last thing I wanted was to be a single parent to my 3 children. I wasn't just afraid; I was terrified. What if I had to raise my children alone for the next 15 years? At that moment, I wasn't sure I had the energy or strength to carry my family through another 15 years of Ron being in prison. Panic was beginning to surpass the grief. I forced myself to focus. I pushed my thoughts about the future aside and began to think about right now.

How will they send Ron back to prison? Will they show up at our home and arrest him? Will they come today - are they on their way right now? I took a few deep, ragged breaths to calm my thinking. As I began to think rationally again, I pulled away from the huddle and sat on the couch. Ron came over and sat next to me, and our sons stood looking at us for direction. "Boys, go finish unloading the van," Ron quietly, but firmly directed them. As they left the room, we held hands and sat in silence for a few minutes absorbing the news. "What now?" I asked. "Will they come here to arrest you?" I did not want our sons to see their father arrested in our home. I needed this home to be our haven. "Can we go somewhere else to stay tonight?" I asked Ron. Ron nodded, "Yes, that is a good idea. Let's pack an overnight bag and leave the house until we know what is going to happen." I went to tell the boys to pack a bag of things for an overnight trip to a local hotel while Ron began to make the dreaded phone calls to family and friends. The entire atmosphere in our house was different. Instead of preparing for a party, it felt like we were now preparing for a funeral. We were going to have to say good-bye to our lives as an intact family and adjust to lives without a husband and father once again.

As we loaded the car, there was no laughter, no talking; the silence was suffocating as we moved our things into the back of the van and began the drive to a nearby hotel. As we pulled up to the hotel, we were greeted by friends who had come to share our sorrow and offer help. Two couples stood nervously in the lobby, watching for our arrival. As we entered the lobby, a good friend grabbed my hand and reassured me through her own tears, "It is going to be OK. God has a plan. I know it may seem like He has abandoned you, but He hasn't." She led me to our hotel room. The room seemed to be out of an old mystery movie. The floral curtains were drawn, two beds covered in the same floral pattern and a simple nightstand were the only furnishings in the room. The pale yellow ceiling fixture seemed to be suppressing the light from intruding on our grief. Everything was surreal. Surely God would not allow this to happen to our family again? No one would ever send an innocent man to prison twice for the same crime, right?

Ron – Bad Advice from Good Friends

I couldn't believe what I was hearing. I couldn't believe I was to go back to prison. My mind was reeling. All I wanted to do was to protect my family. It was hard to breathe. It was even harder to stay in control when all I wanted to do was scream.

We began to get calls from well-meaning friends. More than anything, we wanted to be together. Their advice to us was to grab our children and run to Mexico or Canada and live our lives together as a family. We had really good people giving us really bad advice.

"We can give you a cell phone," someone said, "Don't use yours; they can trace it."

"We have some money for you. We already called a local restaurant and paid for you and your family to eat for the week."

"This is not fair. No one would voluntarily go to prison for something they didn't do. Take your family and move out of the country. We will help you."

We sat on the bed and listened to the condolences and advice from dozens of people. My mom arrived and came and sat with us on the bed. Sensing that words were not needed or wanted, she remained silent. We listened to the counsel of others for several hours before the phone slowed its ringing and all our visitors left. We were alone now. I turned on the TV to divert our sons' attention away from the gravity of our situation and walked over to look out of the only window in the room. The window was just above the vent in the room. The cool air blew against me as I watched people coming and going. They were completely oblivious to my family's trauma. "Nothing stops the motion of life," I thought to myself.

The piercing sound of the hotel phone yanked me back into the room. Cathy and I exchanged a look. Only a few people knew where we were. I picked up the phone and recognized Eric's voice right away. "Ron?" he asked. "Yes. Hey, Eric, any more news?" I responded with my own pressing question. "Actually, I just got off the phone with the judge." He paused. I waited silently. "He has set the date for you to return to prison next week. You will report to the county corrections center and they will transport you from there." I could not respond. "So it is true. I am going to back to prison." I thought about this as I forced myself to answer him. "Thank you for letting me know. I will let Cathy know. Is there anything else I need to know?" I asked as calmly as I could. "I will call you back with the exact time. Ron, I am so sorry this is happening to your family. I trust that you will do the right thing." With that he hung up the phone. I carefully replaced the phone on its cradle and turned to Cathy and my sons. They had turned off the TV and were all looking expectantly at me. "Well, I have a week before I have to return to prison." Before I could finish, Brandon ran into me and wrapped his arms tightly around my chest sobbing. Blake stood up and balled his fists as he stared at the wall. "No. Please, God, no," was all Cathy said. She reached over and gently pushed Blake's hair off of his forehead. The small gesture snapped Blake out of his carefully controlled response. He turned to his mother and wept in her arms while I held his younger brother in mine. "God, you will take care of them, right?" was my only thought.

Cathy – I Will Follow You

I could scarcely believe that we were still living the same day! I had awakened that morning full of excitement, and now here we were grieving the loss of our intact family and Ron's return to prison. As our sons moved away from us and settled into their own space, all eyes turned to Ron. Knowing the answer in my heart, I still couldn't stop myself from asking the question, "What are we going to do?" I caught his eyes and held his gaze as I continued, "Ron, whatever you want to do, I will follow you." He looked away from me and into the eyes of each of his teenage sons. Both Blake and Brandon looked back at him questioningly. We all knew that the decision Ron would make would impact us for the rest of our lives. Whatever course he set us on, our lives were about to take on a new dimension. The balance of our lives was held in his decision. Tears welled up in his eyes. He stood there wiping away his tears as he answered our questions. "Every part of me wants to run. I want to pack up my family and leave.

I want to find a spot where I can take care of you, protect you and provide for you." He paused to look at each of us. Then he continued. "But I cannot do that. I know the right thing to do and I HAVE to do it. The judge could have issued a warrant for my arrest. He could have sent the sheriff to handcuff me and take me back. But he didn't. He gave me a week to report back to prison on my own. When I stood in the courtroom right before he released me, he asked me what I had learned. I told him I had learned to be a man of my word and that was what I wanted to teach my sons. He believed me. This is

> I will return to prison next week because the right thing is always the right thing to do, no matter what the cost.

my opportunity to show you, my sons, what that means. I will return to prison next week because the right thing is always the right thing to do, no matter what the cost. Never, ever forget that, boys." He walked over to Blake and Brandon and grabbed them into his arms and held them tightly.

The rest of that week, we spent time together at a campground just outside of town. We hugged, we played together and we prayed together every moment we could. And we cried. We cried until we thought maybe we couldn't cry anymore. And then, we cried some more. We knew the moments were slipping by and we didn't know when we would get to embrace each other again. No one wanted to go back to being "that family" with the father in prison.

Ron – The Last Day of Freedom

The day before I had to return to prison, we went home. I did all I could to make sure everything was in order before I had to leave, because I didn't know when I would be home again. Fifteen more years loomed over me - over all of us, really, because it was clear that my family was doing time with me. As we went to bed that night, we all lingered together. None of us wanted to end our last night together. More than anything, I wanted to erase the pain from my sons' eyes. As we eventually made our way to bed, I insisted that I get to tuck them each into bed. I had missed the privilege of doing that for than a decade, and I wanted to do it one more time before they grew up into men. Walking back down those stairs was one of the most poignant memories I have of my time with them. Each of them had spent time sharing their hearts and fears with me before I kissed them on their foreheads and tucked the blankets around them. They would be men before I was home again. By returning to prison, I realized I was leading them back into the prison environment as well. I prayed I was leading them into a future filled with possibilities, honor and integrity.

I kissed my wife and climbed into bed next to her. I leaned over and rested my head on her belly and sang to our baby. I hoped my child would recognize my voice when she was born. "I love you, little one. You won't get to hear Daddy's voice very often, but I love you, and I will be thinking of you every day." I returned to my pillow and pulled Cathy into my arms. I held her close to me, breathing in the scent of her hair and trying to tell myself that this embrace would carry us through the next journey, even it is was for fifteen more years. Long after she fell asleep, I laid awake just watching her sleep and praying over her. She would need all the strength that God would provide for her to make it through tomorrow and the coming days. I didn't want to waste a moment of my time with her; she was so beautiful. All the worry and fear was erased from her brow as she slept soundly next to me, holding onto my hand even in her sleep. I could sleep in prison tomorrow.

All too quickly, the sun rose and the clock announced that it was time to prepare for my return to prison. I leaned down to kiss Cathy and tell her, "It is time to wake up, Sweetheart." She opened her eyes and reached over to hold me tightly. Tears ran unchecked down her face. I kissed her salty cheek and rolled out of bed to get the boys up. As I walked into Blake's room, I found him sleeping sweetly. I hated to interrupt his dream with the harsh reality of our day, but walked over to him and touched his arm lightly. He opened his eyes and seeing me, he jumped up quickly, "Did I oversleep?" he asked in a voice thick with sleep. "No, but it is time to get up and get ready for today." I went to Brandon's room and found him already up. He was dressed and standing outside his room. "Hey, Dad. Are you ready for today?" he asked me as he grabbed my hand. I looked at him and replied, "By the grace of God, I will be ready to do what God asks of me." He continued to hold my hand as we walked down the stairs together. I wondered how many fathers had the privilege of holding hands with their 13 year old son. We walked into the living room together and paused to pray for strength to get us through the day.

Cathy – The Trip Back

It took every ounce of determination I had to get out of my bed and get ready to go watch Ron walk back into prison. As we went through our normal morning activities, I couldn't help thinking that maybe at the last minute someone would tell us a mistake had been made. Our friends arrived to take us to the jail right on time. As I opened the door, I felt a twinge of resentment at their intrusion on our last few moments together, but this was also mingled with gratitude for their presence and support. As I walked back into our - now my - bedroom, Ron followed me and drew me into his embrace. We stood there just holding each other, willing time to stop. But time did not stop. As our pastor called out to us to let us know it was time to go, Ron left me physically and emotionally. I felt him pull all of his energy away from me. I knew he needed every ounce of strength he had to be able to walk away from us and back into prison, but the void was so tangible that I almost stumbled as I walked out behind him. I realized I would have to muster every bit of courage I had to keep moving forward.

The trip to the jail went all too fast. As we arrived, I looked at the sea of cars that filled the parking lot and then noticed a group of people who had gathered to show their support for our family. As we walked up to the crowd, they began to applaud us and embrace us. I could barely hold back my tears. The ground was still slightly damp with dew, but the sun was quickly heating the earth so the air was filled with a sweet, summer fragrance. We made our way to the center of the group and looked around us. There were over a hundred people there; small children, teens, young adults, middle-aged adults and even an elderly couple stood around us. They held hands and formed a circle as they began singing Amazing Grace and praying over us. Each of them took turns coming over to us to say farewell to Ron as he prepared to make the walk over to the jail entrance. A guard came out to greet us and instructed us that only a few of us could walk with Ron. I grabbed onto his hand and we began the walk back to prison together. As we approached the facility, the guard turned to us, saying, "This is as far as she can come. You will have to go the rest of the way alone."

He briefly hugged me and then turned to walk the rest of the way alone. I stood there, watching him until he disappeared from sight. Seeing Ron walk back into prison was one of the most difficult things I had ever done, but it was also one of the proudest moments in our marriage. We had passed the biggest test of our character. Human nature considers all the options, but your character makes the final decision. We did the right thing in spite of sorrow, loss, and injustice.

Every marriage and every relationship will face crises. What happens in the midst of those crises depends on the foundation that you have built. Being sent back to prison after serving more than ten years doesn't happen to every family. However, every marriage is riddled with moments of disappointment, disagreement and discouragement.

Tough decisions and life-altering junctures are a part of "normal" family life, whether or not they are obviously so. Without friendship, faithfulness, forgiveness, fairness and fortitude, marriages fail and families fall apart. When the news came that Ron had to return to prison for as many as fifteen more years, divorce was not even a blip on our radar. Although it wasn't clear how we would meet this challenge, we never questioned if we would get through this trial together. We had already developed the character we needed to make our relationship permanent.

When family members learn what to do in times of trial, to make the choice to have the proper response, and are committed to the greater good of their family, they grow stronger because they face the difficulties together. They build immunity against future attacks to their family and develop the tenacity they need to hang onto each other in the midst of the storms. A healthy family experiences challenges just like every other family does, but those challenges make their family stronger. In the midst of difficult times, even if they are a result of bad decisions, the healthy family navigates through the hardship and recognizes that it is only a passing season of their life, not a death sentence. They recover from it stronger than they were before.

The High Fives are the Principles That Can Build Your Family

Learning and practicing the five principles will transform your family into a loving, strong, healthy family that can survive the trials of life and emerge closer together as a result.

⌒ **Friendship** – Sharing experiences is what creates friendship. Honestly share the deepest parts of yourself in order to create and build friendships in your family. Be a friend. Friendship is the chief virtue of family relationships. It is born out of the most basic social need – which is to share.

⌒ **Faithfulness** - affirming your family's intrinsic value, demonstrating steady allegiance and fulfilling your duty to protect, love and defend them. Remaining loyal in the face of temptation is what builds faithfulness and creates the trust that is vital to solidify the friendship and help it grow. Without faithfulness, friendship is impossible. Faithfulness is the foundation that allows one person to trust another. When it is present it frees all a person's relationships to deal openly and honestly – in other words to be willing to share.

⌒ **Forgiveness** – The ability to move beyond the offenses from others and experience the freedom that comes from releasing others for the larger purpose of family strength. Forgiving others and seeking forgiveness from them will heal wounds and bring about reconciliation and greater levels of sharing and meaning in your friendships. It is a strange paradox that we all fail - but that we all seem to have a hard time forgiving other people when they fail us. Failure is inevitable. But refusing to forgive others makes having successful, stable, long-term relationships impossible.

⌒ **Fairness** – Learning to see in our circumstances the opportunity to use effective communication skills to resolve conflict and strengthen our relationships. Looking past our own expectations allows

153

us to extend fairness and allows relationships to survive the most painful trials. Everyone thinks that they are right and justified. The challenge of practicing fairness is in looking past our circumstances so that we can focus on others and extend fairness to them. Fairness means being committed to living by a certain set of rules. Learn to use effective communication skills to work lovingly with others through difficult circumstances.

    ✎ **Fortitude** – The strength of mind, will and purpose that enables a family to courageously face danger and endure pain or adversity together. The commitment to the higher good of building the health of your family will give you the strength to consistently choose to have the proper response to your circumstances and do the little things that are right, even when you do not feel like it. As fortitude grows stronger, it becomes the ability to stand your ground in the face of danger. Whatever your circumstances are, fortitude is a discipline. It is composed of three parts: having a clear sense of what is essential, choosing to do what is right instead of compromising or settling for something inferior, and a wholehearted commitment to pursuing the higher goal.

Building a strong and healthy marriage and family requires courage. You must have the courage to learn and then apply the information and skills that help you grow stronger, but you must also find the courage to be different and unique and to overcome those who might discourage you from achieving this goal, no matter how well intentioned they are.

Take the First Step to Build Your Family's Health!

We are so happy to share what we have learned over these last 22 years of working to build and strengthen our own family. As a result of the things we have endured, we have grown into a family that is strong enough to help others. We have had the opportunity to work with thousands of other families to bring them to a new awareness of the peace, hope and strength that can be yours too.

Own It!

Own your situation. Whether your family is already fairly healthy or falling apart at the seams, there is always plenty of room for growth! There are no perfect families, so start implementing the High Fives to make your family permanent and healthy. Whatever trials you are facing, start by owning the situation. Acknowledge how your actions have contributed to the present state of the health or ill-health of your family and how you intend to adjust your behavior in order to strengthen your family. Let the rest of your family know what you've learned, and begin building the bridge to the rest of your family members by sharing honestly.

Do not worry if the other members of your family are reluctant to join you. It's OK if others don't get on board right away, or if it takes a long time for them to show an interest. The key is to help them understand the different choices that you are beginning to make in your life and your commitment to helping the family grow. You need to let them know that what is motivating you to change is your commitment to them. Remember that a healthy family is unlocked by a willingness to share – so look for opportunities to share the things that mean the most to the other members of your family. Look to create opportunities that put you in a position to express friendship and to share the joys, sorrows and challenges of life.

We are here to help you, no matter what you are going through! In addition to this book, we offer products and services that can support you and help to reach each of the members of your family and encourage them to actively work for renewed health in your family's relationships.

Additional Resources to Strengthen Your Marriage and Family

Prison Fellowship – Angel Tree Program
http://www.prisonfellowship.org/programs/angel-tree/

Relationship Help Centers
http://marriagehelpcenters.com/

Smart Marriages
http://www.smartmarriages.com

National Association for Relationship and Marriage Education
https://www.narme.org

Dr. Rozario Slack
http://www.rozarioslack.com/

Couple Communication
http://www.couplecommunication.com/

Better Marriages
http://bettermarriages.org

Marc Payan
http://www.payanx.com

10 Great Dates - Marriage Alive
http://www.marriagealive.com/10Dates

If you are looking for additional resources to strengthen your marriage and family, the websites above will provide you with a plethora of materials, information, and opportunities to invest in your relationship.